trade
SECRETS
GARDENING

GARDENING

Katherine Lapworth

ORION

First published in 1999 by Orion Books Ltd

Orion House, 5 Upper St Martin's Lane,
London WC2H 9EA

Copyright © Maverick TV Ltd 1999

Maverick TV has asserted its right to
be identified as the proprietor of this work.

A CIP catalogue record for this book is
available from the British Library.

ISBN 0 75281 816 3

Printed and bound in Great Britain
by Clays Ltd, St Ives plc

Contents

Foreword

From rolling acres to a few pots on the window sill, gardeners have cultivated their own particular plots with love, dedication and passion. From these sons and daughters of the soil have come an extraordinary range of trade secrets.

Gardeners are generally thought to be extremely nice people; if some of these tips are anything to go by, they're galloping eccentrics too. But if spanking a tree or peeing in your orchard means healthy, vigorous growth and abundant crops, then who are we to complain? Just don't let the neighbours catch you at it.

From the eminently sensible and practical to some wilder flights of fancy, we have included hints and tips to make your garden grow.

'All gardeners know better than other gardeners.'   *Chinese proverb*

'There can be no other occupation like gardening in which, if you were to creep behind someone at their work, you would find them smiling.'   *Mirabel Osler*

'The story of mankind started in a garden and ended in revelations.'   *Oscar Wilde*

'The true gardener, like a true artist, is never satisfied.'   *H. E. Bates*

'Nothing grows in our garden, only washing. And babies.'
Dylan Thomas Under Milk Wood

SEEDS AND PLANTING OUT

....

'Perennials are the ones that grow like weeds, biennials are the ones that die this year instead of next and hardy annuals are the ones that never come up at all.'
Katharine Whitehorn

To collect seeds,

put the ripe seed head in a paper bag and shake.

When storing seeds,

make sure moisture doesn't ruin them. Keep them in an airtight tin. As an added precaution, wrap some milk powder in tissue, seal with a rubber band and leave it in the tin.

Seeds in pods should not be stored in airtight containers.

They need a flow of air round them. When the pods are dry, you can remove the seeds and put them in a paper bag.

Small seeds can stick to your hands when you're sowing.

Keep your hands cool by running cold water over your wrists and then drying your hands thoroughly before you start.

Dry seeds by putting them on a piece of kitchen paper
and leaving to dry thoroughly. If seeds are still damp, they may start to rot or germinate.

The best place to store seeds
is in the fridge.

Always label your seeds;
some will keep for ages while others only last a year.

Sow seeds evenly.
Punch holes in the top of a jam jar or coffee jar and screw the top on; use this to shake out the seeds.

The smaller the seeds, the shallower they should be sown.

Mix small seeds with sand
for easy planting.

Plant seedlings in bits of old gutter
— they are easy to slide off the end for re-potting.

For an alternative seed starter, use tea-bags.

Thin delicate seedlings with a pair of tweezers.
This doesn't disturb the roots of the remaining seedlings.

Use your linen cupboard to propagate seeds
that don't need much light. Cover seed trays with clingfilm and check daily. As soon as the first seedlings appear, remove the trays.

Conserve moisture – cover seedling pots with clingfilm;
this keeps out draughts and ensures that the temperature remains constant. Take the clingfilm off from time to time to prevent too much moisture building up.

An old sieve is ideal
for getting compost for seeds into trays.

Use white sand to mark
out the areas where you are going to
sow your seeds.

You don't have to scatter seeds randomly.
If you sow them in straight lines, you
will be able to distinguish between
them and the weeds as they grow.

Make a mini greenhouse.
Cut off the top of a plastic drinks bottle
and place over your seedlings.

**Alternatively, use a clear plastic bag as a
temporary greenhouse;**
support it with sticks and secure with a
rubber band.

If you use a propagator for seedlings,
make sure you wipe the inside surface
regularly to remove any condensation.
Too much condensation cuts down
the amount of light reaching the
seedlings.

If the light levels are low
where your seeds are growing, stand
the pots of seedlings on kitchen foil
so that they benefit from the reflected
light.

To separate very small seedlings,
use an old fork to lift them and divide
them carefully.

Settle small seeds into the compost
by wetting them with a plant mister.

To avoid disturbing the roots of plants,
roll newspaper strips into tubes. Fill
with compost and moisten before
sowing seeds into each one. Plant out
the tubes and the roots will grow down
through the newspaper.

The best time to sow grass seed
for a lawn is September. If you miss
this date, you can start the seeds in late
March or early April.

Always sow grass seed on calm, dry days.

Sow lawn seeds using a plant pot
with holes in the bottom as a shaker.

Once you've sown grass seed,
gently rake over some soil to protect it
from birds. This will help to give it a
good start.

**When your grass seeds are a few inches
high,**
you should clip (rather than mow)
them. After this, you can roll the
lawn and then use your lawnmower.

**If you are planning to plant seeds with hard
coats,**
soak them in water overnight. This
will give them a head start when you
plant them.

Always dry seeds before storing them;
    use paper towels or newspaper.

To avoid damping off in seed boxes,
    always use seedling compost and
    never garden soil. Don't reuse compost
    either.

**Use the black plastic bases of drinks bottles
as seed trays**
    – they already have drainage holes cut
    into them and are ideal for the task.

Collect seeds from flowers;
    it's a lot cheaper than going out and
    buying them in packets.

**Cut up old magazines and make seed
packets.**

**Empty film canisters make excellent
containers**
    for storing seeds.

Cover seed trays with clingfilm

to prevent the compost from drying out while the seeds germinate.

Seed vegetables in the clean plastic containers

from ready-cooked meals.

Instead of using pots or boxes to grow your seedlings,

plant them in soil blocks. The advantage is that you can plant them straight out as soon as the roots emerge. Take a short length of plastic piping, 2–3 in/5–7.5 cm wide. Find a glass bottle that fits inside snugly. Stand the tube on a flat surface and fill with compost mixture. Pound down with the bottle several times. Lift off with a twisting motion. You are left with a solid soil block.

Cover a piece of cardboard with silver foil and place it behind a seedling.

Foil reflects light from the window onto the plants, helping them to grow.

Grow your own pansies
by sowing the seeds any time from spring until late autumn. Secure some polythene over them to conserve moisture, speed up germination and protect from pests.

To help sweet pea seeds germinate,
soak them in warm water overnight and then sow them outside in the autumn.

Sweet peas need full sun
so don't hide them away in the shade.

Swop cuttings with other gardeners.

Nobody likes getting into a cold bed and seeds are no different.
Warm the soil the day before you plant by putting a dustbin liner over the soil and holding it in place with stones.

Try to avoid sowing in cold, damp conditions
> – you don't want the seeds to rot before they've had a chance to start growing. Delay sowing until conditions improve.

Tie up delicate climbers with old tights
> cut into strips.

When planting a herbaceous border,
> space tall plants 3 ft/90 cm or so apart and dwarf plants at least 1 ft/30 cm apart.

To support your herbaceous plants,
> pull a coat hanger into a square and hook onto supporting canes.

When you have divided your perennials,
> you may be left with spare plants; use them in containers as well as other parts of the garden.

To support small plants,
remove the inner part of a ballpoint
pen and use the transparent outer skin
as a support.

When planting a shrub in dry soil,
put a pot of gravel down by the roots.
When you water it, the water should go
straight through to the roots.

Always check the roots of a plant.
If they are all knotted up and
congested, soak the roothall in water
for a few hours, tease the roots out and
then plant it.

In hot weather,
line a pot with damp paper before
potting up a plant. This conserves
moisture.

To kick start woody cuttings,
slit the end of the stem and put a grain
of wheat into the cut. As the wheat
germinates, it encourages the root of
the cutting to form.

Split the contents of a grow bag into four pots

rather than using the three holes. This will give you one extra plant and they will be much healthier because the soil is looser.

Before moving a plant,

water the ground it's coming from thoroughly for several days.

When moving a plant,

tie up any loose stems or branches. This makes it easier to carry and reduces the risk of bits and pieces snapping off.

After moving a plant,

cut back the foliage to reduce stress from moisture loss.

If there is a delay before replanting,

wrap the roots of the plant in a plastic bag to keep the moisture in.

After transplanting an evergreen shrub,
spray the foliage every day for two
weeks.

**Cut up old margarine tubs and use them to
label plants.**

**The bottom of an old washing-powder
bottle makes a very effective scoop.**

**Don't stick too rigidly to a planting
timetable.**
Try sowing spring-sown annuals in the
autumn. If it works, you can often get a
much longer flowering period out of
them.

Use annual climbers to cover a bare trellis
while the slower-growing plants get a
chance to establish themselves.

Try growing a cutting from a shrub
by bending a low branch over and
pegging it into the ground. Within a
few weeks you can often find you've
got a new plant growing apace.

When planting out,
make sure that the stem base isn't any
deeper than it was before.

Can't bend down to sow seeds?
Use a drainpipe or hose and drop the
seeds down through it.

**Put used gun cartridges over the ends of
canes**
so you don't blind yourself!

Alternatively,
if shooting isn't your bag and you don't
have cartridges to hand, try a ping-pong
ball instead.

When tying canes together,
secure them temporarily with an
elastic band. Now your hands are free
to tie the canes in position.

To stop larger seedlings from wilting in the sun,
make them little hats out of
newspaper. Weigh down the rim with
stones to stop them blowing away.

**Remember to water plants ten minutes
before you dig the holes for them.**

**If your shrubs are getting too leggy, grow
climbers like clematis over them.**

Roses love a sunny position.

**Bare-rooted roses can be planted in early
autumn**
to the end of March. Container-grown
roses can be planted at any time of the
year.

When planting roses,
make sure the budding point above the roots is slightly below the surface of the soil.

Always prune roses after planting
to encourage growth from the base.

Never plant roses in soil where other roses have previously been grown for five years
or more. Roses can't thrive in poor soil.

Don't plant roses under trees;
they need air to be healthy.

Before planting small alpines,
wrap the roots in moist tissue then place in a crevice. This will protect the roots and give the plant a good start in life.

Weigh a new pond plant down with several large stones.
This will keep the roots beneath the soil and the plant in position.

Deep-water plants, like waterlilies, can be planted up in old washing-up bowls.

Use a heavy soil and cover with gravel to keep in place. Put the bowl in a shallow part of the pond to start with and then move it into deeper water in a couple of weeks.

Spring-flowering bulbs like narcissi are ideal to fill in the gaps in a newly planted border.

They look at their most effective just at the time when all the other plants aren't doing much.

Plants with a blue, silver or grey leaf generally like to go in the warm part of the garden.

Don't plant plants that are in flower.

No one wants to move while they're making love ... and it's the same for a plant!

Planting a climber at an angle will encourage it to grow towards its support.

It will also prevent the roots from being too sheltered and away from rain.

Don't buy plants after a very cold spell

– their roots may have been badly affected.

Annuals, perennials and bulbs are great at filling in gaps in borders.

Grow fragrant flowers round the area where you keep your dustbins

– try honeysuckle, jasmine and roses. They'll not only make the area look more attractive but it will smell better too.

Dense planting round the bin area in the summer

will help to cut down the strong pong.

Grow house plants from the green tops of fresh pineapples and carrots.

Just cut off the bit you intend to eat and push the green end into some compost. When your pineapple starts to grow, cover the pot with a clear plastic bag, secured by a rubber band, to give it a kick start.

Containers don't just have to sit on patios or walls.

They are useful when it comes to filling in gaps in your borders as well.

When planting up a terracotta or stone container,

water both it and the plants before planting to stop the compost from drying out.

If your container is quite tall,

make sure you stabilize it by putting large stones or rubble in the bottom before planting up.

When planting up a tall container,
save compost by planting up a smaller
pot which will fit into the top of the
container.

**Don't put a plant that will grow a lot in a
barrel- or urn-shaped container.**
You will only be able to remove it by
smashing the pot.

Some clematis can be planted in containers
which make them ideal for small
gardens. Try Arctic Queen or
Fireworks.

When planting up hanging baskets,
wrap plants in pieces of polythene
shaped into a cone. This will protect
the rootball when you pull it through
the basket. Once the plant is in
position, remove the polythene.

**Alternative linings for hanging baskets are
newspaper, knitwear or blanket weed.**

Make your own hanging basket

– use an old colander or large sieve
with some chains attached.

Alternatively,

large catering containers may not look
attractive but plant them up with
trailing plants to hide the sides and you
have a handy pot.

For a different hanging basket,

transform unwanted lampshades by
turning them upside down and planting
them up.

Bulbs should be planted

at a depth of between three and five
times their height.

When planting bulbs,

use an apple corer to make holes in the
ground.

When choosing bulbs,

'big is best'.

Most bulbs look best planted in informal groups

of odd numbers.

Save yourself time and effort

– plant several bulbs in one large hole rather than having lots of little holes with one bulb in each.

Short of space?

Plant tulips and daffodils at double the normal depth and sow annuals on top.

Plant snowdrops and winter aconites

once they have stopped flowering but still have their leaves; they establish themselves much better in this form.

Planting bulbs in baskets

means you can easily lift them when they start to fade and leave them out of sight while the foliage dies down.

Plant bulbs under deciduous shrubs.

They will flower and fill the bare patch of earth. When the shrub's in leaf, it will hide the dying plants.

A container for bulbs should have lots of holes for drainage.

A pond basket is a good alternative.

New water plants often contain tiny duckweed plants

which, once *in situ*, can multiply at an alarming rate. Always rinse all new pond plants under the tap before planting.

Always line the baskets of pond plants

to keep soil round the roots. A bit of old sacking is just fine.

Adding floating plants to a pond

not only makes it look attractive but will help prevent the water getting too warm and give shelter to the pond's inhabitants.

Autumn is the time to divide congested water plants.
Remove any weak or damaged sections before replanting.

Limestone is the best basis for a rock garden.
If you prefer sandstone, go for stones that aren't too weathered and crumbled.

If you haven't got room for a rockery,
make a trough garden. You can use a variety of containers as long as they are at least 4 in/10 cm deep.

Plant slow-growing varieties of rock plants together
so that they don't get swamped by their faster-growing cousins.

To help your carnation cutting take root,
place a grain of rice alongside the cutting when planting up.

If you have a sloping garden,

make sure you use plants that don't need much looking after. They can be difficult to get to.

It can often be damper at the bottom of a slope

so make sure you plant moisture-loving plants there.

Plant annuals on cool days or in a shady area.

Avoid extreme temperatures. The best time to plant is in the early evening which gives the plants time to settle before the midday heat.

Acidic plants can be grown in alkaline soil.

Collect leaves from your garden and place in plastic bags. In the spring, dig a large hole, line with the dead leaves and place the plant (now cocooned by the leaves) into the hole. Fill and water as normal.

When planting a tree,

cut off a bit of old hose and place
one end next to the roots. When you
fill in the hole, leave the other end
pointing out of the soil. Then when
you water, it will go directly to the
roots.

**Check the growing habits of a tree before
planting it.**

Some roots can undermine large
structural foundations (especially if
you have a clay-based soil).

To avoid tree roots damaging drains,

find out the ultimate height of the tree
you want. Then plant it at least one
and a half times this distance from
your buildings and drains.

If your garden is dominated by trees,

use plants that like woodland
conditions.

For a natural woodland look,
go for plants that are self-seeding, have small flowers and simple foliage.

Don't forget to water plants under trees.
The leaves and branches act like an umbrella and keep most of the rain off them.

The further away from a tree you go,
the more light the plants on the ground will receive, so plant accordingly.

When planting under trees,
be careful not to damage the tree roots.

To attract wildlife onto your land,
plant mountain ash or alder. They are fast-growing trees and produce lots of fruit for the birds.

Make sure newly planted trees have a good start in life

by providing shelter for them as they grow and by keeping them clear of weeds.

Protect a young clematis

by planting it several inches deeper than it was in its container and surrounding the base with a cylinder of cardboard or plastic to prevent slugs from nibbling at it. Put some grease round the top of the cylinder to stop slugs and snails from climbing over it.

You can give a new lease of life to a hawthorn hedge

by bending some of the pliable stems down into the soil. Secure them using metal hooks. In time, they will take root and start to fill out the bottom of the hedge.

When planting against a brick wall,
remember that the wall will take
moisture from the soil so choose
your plants accordingly (*Aquifolium,
Euonymus, Alchemilla mollis* are
good choices).

**Remove flowers and large leaves from
a perennial when planting.**
This helps to give it a good start in
life and prevents moisture loss.

COMPOST AND FERTILIZER

....

'All really grim gardeners possess a keen sense of humus.'
W. C. Sellar and R. J. Yeatman

Make your own fertilizer
– boil nettle leaves and leave to steep for 24 hours.

Urine is a great fertilizer
if you dilute it ten to one.

When you clean your coffee maker,
sprinkle a thin layer of coffee grounds onto the soil surfaces of your potted plants. As the coffee grounds are high in nitrogen and other nutrients, they will decompose into a slightly acid-forming nutrient source.

Horse manure, cow dung and compost
make a good fertilizer.

Pigeon poo, and rabbit and goat droppings
all make good compost activators.

If you're friendly with a brewery,
try getting some of their spent hops to use as a soil conditioner. Use them as mulch or compost.

Gardeners living near the sea
have a ready source of rich fertilizer.
Seaweed can be used straight away or
put into the compost heap.

Collect sheep droppings in a hessian sack
then suspend the sack in a barrel of
water. Use the water as liquid fertilizer.

Wood ash is a useful fertilizer
and also deters beetles and other
insects if spread round your plants.

Comfrey leaves are rich in potassium.
You can harvest the leaves, put them
to soak in some water and use the
liquid as fertilizer, or let them rot
down before putting on the garden.

To improve the texture of the soil,
add a handful of chopped bracken
when planting. Bracken is slightly
acidic so don't use it with lime-loving
plants.

Leaf-mould, cocoa fibre and organic matter

will all improve the soil's moisture retention, drainage and texture.

Make your own leaf-mould.

Collect the leaves and put them in a large bin bag. Make some holes in the side of the bag and fold the top over. Weigh down with a brick and leave for 6 to 12 months.

Apply humus mulch at the right time

– when the soil is warm and moist. May is ideal.

Keep grass cuttings.

Throw them onto the compost heap (or into a black bag) and cover with a piece of carpet until they've mulched down.

To preserve nutrients in grass,

only cut the top third of the grass and leave the other two thirds; that way, the grass keeps its nutrients and doesn't die.

An inexpensive alternative to mulch

is wet newspaper placed onto wet soil round a shrub. Cover the paper with soil to disguise it.

Use hedge trimmings in compost;

but don't put them into a compost heap if you know that the hedge is diseased.

Don't feed a plant if it's been suffering from lack of water.

It won't be able to absorb the fertilizer properly.

Make your own mini compost heap.

Use plastic bin bags (heavy duty ones if possible) and put all your kitchen waste, old newspapers and garden trimmings in them. Make a few holes in the side and turn the contents over every now and again. Use when everything has rotted down.

Alternatively, use chicken wire held in place by wooden stakes.

Cover the compost heap with a piece of old carpet.

Natural fibre knitted items,

such as jumpers and cardigans, can be cut up and added to your compost. Don't use your mum's cashmere sweater though!

Alternatively, old feather pillows make a good compost ingredient.

Old carpet can be used in compost

as well as being an effective lid on your compost heap. Chop it up into small squares.

Always layer your compost.

Try not to add too much of any ingredient at one time and try to alternate a moist ingredient (like grass clippings) with something drier.

When adding layers to your compost heap,
don't add more than 6 in/15 cm per layer.

Alternatively, bury small amounts of rubbish and clippings around the garden.
The worms will then take over and do the composting for you.

Accelerate your compost
by mixing green manure into it.

Alternatively, put some fresh horse manure inside
and you'll soon be rewarded with wonderful organic compost.

If the weather gets hot,
give your compost a drink of water. This encourages the ingredients to break down.

When it's cold,
> make sure your compost wraps up nice and warm. If it gets too cold, it won't rot down.

To construct your own composter,
> put some holes in the side and base of an old dustbin and stand it on some bricks for drainage.

Make sure you put some carbon in your compost
> – use cereal packets, egg boxes and so on. These will give the compost some bulk.

Create a cheap mulch for the garden
> by shredding any left-over bits of wood.

Using peat is not environmentally friendly
> so investigate the alternatives.

Don't throw banana skins away;
> place them round the bottom of your roses for great fertilizer.

Fertilize your azaleas and camellias
by placing used tea-bags round their
roots.

Also, azaleas love the odd drink
of 2 pints/1.2 litres water mixed with
two tablespoons of white vinegar.

To encourage geranium growth,
keep all your eggshells in a bucket of
water. After a few weeks, remove the
eggshells, and water your geraniums
with the liquid.

**Put crushed eggshells in the bottom of a
planting hole**
for extra calcium. Eggshells are
alkaline so don't use for plants that
like acid soil.

When growing leeks,
give them some stout to drink to
stimulate their growth.

Alternatively, try some soot.

It works just as well.

Roses need to be planted in well-prepared soil

so give them a good start with well-rotted farmyard manure.

In the summer, mulch rose beds

after it has rained.

Perk up your plants

by feeding them with half a can of non-diet Coca-Cola.

Make your own liquid fertilizer from nettles.

Put freshly picked nettles into a large bucket. Cover with water (around 18 pints/10 litres water to 2 lb/1 kg nettles) and seal with clingfilm. Leave for a few weeks, stirring now and again. When the nettles have rotted down, strain the mixture into a bucket. Dilute the liquid with water about ten times before using.

Alternatively, soak nettles together with thistles

for a few months and use that as a fertilizer.

If you can't be bothered to dig in organic matter,

spread it over the soil in the autumn and leave the winter weather to break it down for you.

Improve the texture of your soil

by digging in coarse sand and gravel. Avoid using builder's sand because it can contain harmful contaminants.

If you want to improve the alkalinity of your soil,

use mushroom compost.

When planting near a wall,

it's worth remembering that the soil there gets less rain and so would benefit from a little extra help. Dig in some well-rotted manure before planting.

Use leaf-mould in the soil when building a rockery.

The humus content keeps the moisture in dry periods and allows for easy drainage in wet weather.

When planting up a trough garden,

put in a layer of leaf-mould and then a layer of charcoal between the drainage material at the bottom and the compost on top.

WEEDS

....

'A weed is a plant whose virtues have not yet been discovered.'
Ralph Waldo Emerson

Don't throw away the salted boiling water
that you've cooked your potatoes in.
Use it as a weedkiller on paths and
drives.

To deter weeds,
sprinkle sand on garden paths.

Cut nettles down to the ground
the moment they appear. Under
constant persecution, they will
eventually give up.

Wear a woolly glove over a rubber glove.
Dip your hand into weedkiller and then
stroke the plants.

Use old carpets as mulch to kill weeds.
It's a non-toxic way of deterring weeds.

Cover garden beds with pine bark
to prevent weeds.

Leaving soil uncovered will only encourage weeds.

> Use some form of ground cover, either a mulch or ground-cover plants.

Use Epsom salts to kill weeds.

When tackling bindweed,

> grow it up a cane before applying weedkiller. This way you won't damage other garden plants.

Remember this rhyme:

> Thistles cut in May return next day
> Thistles cut in June come up soon
> But cut them in July
> And they are sure to die.

When weeding,

> attach your rings to a safety pin and pin them to your clothing so you don't lose them.

Rake up the moss from your lawn
    and keep it in a damp place to use in
    hanging baskets.

Use an old potato peeler to dig up weeds
    from your lawn.

Alternatively, use an old kitchen knife
    to dig up dandelions and daisies from a
    lawn. Keep the blade vertical and cut in
    a circle round the weed. Pull out with
    the root intact.

**A camomile lawn should always be weeded
by hand.**

Dandelions and plantain don't like salt
    – so use the odd pinch now and again to
    keep them away.

To slaughter stubborn weeds,
    blast them with a mixture of gin and
    detergent.

If you're using a weedkiller,
> protect your plants with a sheet of
> cardboard or a bin liner as you are
> spraying.

**To make your own funnel to administer
weedkiller more easily,**
> cut off the top of a plastic drinks bottle.
> You can then throw it away after
> you've used it.

**Some weeds will absorb chemicals more
easily**
> if you crush their foliage before
> applying the weedkiller. So stamp
> your feet!

To get rid of green slime from your patio,
> scrub with a stiff brush and soapy
> water.

Weeds like water too
> so remove them regularly and make
> sure your plants get the moisture
> instead.

In hot weather,
> leave uprooted weeds on the soil
> surface. They'll act as a layer of
> mulch and help retain moisture
> in the soil.

**Stop your neighbour's weeds from creeping
into your garden.**
> Dig a trench 1 ft/30 cm deep alongside
> the fence. Line on one side with
> dustbin bags and then replace the soil.

**Use an old colander to remove algae
from ponds.**

**A good way to prevent algae from growing
in your pond**
> is to stuff the leg of a pair of old tights
> with barley straw. Tie both ends
> securely, attach a weight to one end
> and then submerge in the pond.

Keep pond surfaces clear of fallen leaves.
    If you leave them, they can cause a
    build-up of toxic gases which can kill
    fish and wildlife.

Use an old net curtain to cover your pond in winter.
    This will catch falling leaves for you.
    Remember to shake it out regularly.

Blanket weed is best removed from your pond using a stick.
    Wind it round and round as if it were
    candyfloss.

To remove duckweed from a pond,
    draw a plank vertically across the
    surface and then remove the weed
    using an old colander or sieve.

Always bury duckweed in a hole
    or put it in the dustbin or on the
    compost heap. It's a tough little thing
    and can spread easily.

Keep weeds down
> by planting up the gaps and cracks
> between paving stones with seeds of
> hardy annuals.

Alternatively, ensure that the grouting between paving stones is done properly
> in the first place.

PESTS

....

*'We have descended into the garden
and caught three hundred slugs. How
I love the mixture of the beautiful and
the squalid in gardening. It makes it so
lifelike.'*
Evelyn Underhill

Slugs hate seaweed;
use it on your beds as a great fertilizer
as well.

Stop snails and slugs in their tracks.
Smear petroleum jelly on the rim of
flower pots to stop your plants getting
attacked.

Stop slugs coming into the house
– lay a line of salt across the doorway.
The slugs won't cross the line.

Half a grapefruit left upside down
makes a great slug trap.

Another slug deterrent is to scatter crushed eggshells
round your tender plants.

Slug pubs work wonders.
Cut slug-sized holes in the lid of a
cottage cheese tub, fill the tub with
beer and sink it into the ground.

Alternatively, pour some beer round your favourite plants
to keep slugs away.

Wave goodbye to slugs
by smearing lettuce or cabbage leaves
with lard and leaving them dotted
around the garden. When they are
covered with slugs, pick them up and
throw them away.

Slugs don't like strands of horsehair rope
laid across the soil surface.

Holly twigs are also a slug deterrent.

Encourage frogs and toads into the garden;
they love slugs! Victorian gardeners
used to keep a couple of toads in the
greenhouse to keep the slug population
down.

Entice slugs from your drain

– pour turpentine down the drain. The slugs will come out and you can get rid of them permanently.

Alternatively, try putting a piece of board or hardboard down on the ground.

The slugs will hide underneath it to get out of the sun. When you've got a fair crop, lift the board up and wreak vengeance!

Protect delicate seedlings from slugs

by surrounding them with the cardboard centres of loo rolls, or milk cartons with the tops and bottoms cut off.

Mix wood ash with slaked lime and spread around your seedlings

to stop slugs from attacking them.

To stop mice and birds eating your peas,
soak the packet of peas in paraffin and leave for 24 hours. Cut off the end of the packet, drain the peas and then plant when needed.

Garden pests can be controlled using Jeyes Fluid.
Pop some in your spray bottle and use on blackfly and greenfly.

Alternatively, use Jeyes Fluid in your watering can
to combat slugs and snails.

If you are being plagued by blackfly,
just sprinkle some soil from the base of the plant over the pests.

Pinch out the tips of broad beans
to discourage blackfly.

When using weedkiller,
be careful not to get any on your boots or gardening shoes. You don't want to tramp it all over the garden.

Protect your vegetable patch with an 'instant snake'.
Take an old piece of garden hose, about the length of a snake (remember, we're not in the Amazon so don't go over the top!) and wind it on the ground and round your plants. Cats and birds will stay away at the sight of the 'snake'.

To catch codling moths,
wrap a piece of old sacking round the trunk of an apple tree in the summer. The moths will crawl into the sacking and you can then take it down and burn it.

A bruised garlic clove
left at the entrance of a wasps' nest will clear it.

Keep pests out of the shed and house
– spray insect repellent across the edge
of the door and along the window-sill.

When the birds have flown,
take down their nest and either throw
it away or burn it. Nests are great
places for insects to live in.

Make your own bird scarers
by sticking feathers in the ground
amongst the vegetables. Being
territorial creatures, they'll keep off
another bird's patch.

For a cheap and effective bird scarer,
cut flaps in a plastic bottle, put it over
the top of a cane and secure it with a
nail. The wind will make the bottle go
round which will scare the birds away.

**Use the tape from a broken cassette fixed to
the top of bamboo canes as a bird scarer.**

Discourage birds

by criss-crossing black thread over the area you want to protect. It won't be an eyesore but will stop them from landing.

String milk bottle tops on pieces of string

and then suspend them between sticks driven in the ground. Birds will stay away.

Mix up your own insect spray

from a mixture of water and a little washing-up liquid.

Alternatively, make your own spray

by soaking 3 oz/75 g of chopped onion or garlic in two teaspoons of liquid paraffin for 24 hours. Strain the liquid. Mix with a solution of ¼ oz/10 g soft soap in 1 pint/600 ml of warm water. Shake well. Dilute two tablespoons to 1 pint/600 ml of water and fill your spray bottle. Go get 'em!

To get rid of pests from plants,
spray with garlic tea.

Soak nettle and wormwood leaves in a bucket of water
for a week and then use the water as a spray to control aphids.

Soak elder leaves in a bucket of water
for a week and then use the liquid as a spray to control flea beetle.

Soak tomato leaves in a bucket of water
for a week and use the water as a spray to control caterpillar damage to cabbages.

Planting marigolds round the base of a rose bush
can deter rose pests.

Alternatively, growing alliums and catmint
next to your roses will help combat aphids.

Use a soft brush to sweep away aphids
 from rose bushes.

To protect your dahlias from earwigs,
 dip a piece of cotton wool in machine
 oil and tie it round the stem of the
 plant (about 1 ft/30 cm from the
 ground). Tie some round any canes as
 well to stop them climbing up to reach
 the flowers.

To stop earwigs nibbling your fruit and veg,
 place an empty matchbox, half open,
 at the top of the plant canes.

If earwigs are causing a problem on your fruit trees,
 tie some cloths round the branches.
 Once a week, take the cloths off the
 branches and shake them out – well
 away from your garden.

The gardeners of yore used a sheep's hoof, upended on a cane, to trap earwigs.

Marigolds attract hoverflies
which control pests as well as repel
whitefly. Grow some in your hanging
baskets, grow bags and vegetable plots.

**Marigolds, nasturtiums and flax will help
protect potatoes**
from pests.

**Alternatively, growing peas next to your
potatoes**
is thought to deter pests.

**To clear flying insects and their eggs from
your greenhouse,**
use a vacuum cleaner.

**Sink empty bottles up to their necks in the
garden.**
Moles don't like the sound of the wind
across the empty tops.

Stick a child's windmill in the ground near a mole's run.
> The wind causes vibrations to run down the stem and into the run which disturbs the mole.

Alternatively, line the bottom of their run with gorse.
> Moles hate having their noses pricked.

To deter moles,
> put mothballs or orange peel down their run.

Moles hate any foul-smelling liquid
> – try pouring cleaning fluid or old flower water down the entrance to mole runs.

Alarm moles into leaving.
> Set an alarm clock and push it down the mole hole. Once it goes off, the moles should leave home.

Alternatively, plant caper-spurge near a mole run.

Some people consider it a weed but moles hate the smell.

Moles don't get along with cats.

Try putting sweet chewing gum into mole holes.

Some say the moles eat the gum and it clogs their digestive systems.

Woodlice like the damp.

Sprinkle talcum powder around the affected surfaces. The woodlice will soon look for alternative accommodation.

Woodlice are fond of house plants

so don't put plants on window-sills and ledges; it will only encourage the woodlice to come into the house.

Little spiders grow up...

into big spiders. Plug up any holes in outside walls, however tiny, to stop the little ones from crawling in.

Rhubarb leaves help to deter pests.

There's an old country custom

of lining baskets of freshly picked strawberries and blackberries with elder leaves which are a great insect deterrent.

Daisy-like flowering plants are very attractive to insects

who will help you combat pests and aid in pollination. Plants such as *Alyssum, Campanula, Geranium, Gypsophila* and *Salvia* are ideal.

Get rid of ants

by placing half a squeezed orange where the ants will find it. Soon the peel will be full of ants and you can then dispose of them suitably. Placing the peel where the birds will find it is a good idea – they will eat the ants.

Place banana skins around plants and rose bushes

outside the house to stop ants from coming in.

Alternatively, just sprinkle around some dried tansy.

Ants avoid any surface that has been treated,

so keep them out by drawing a chalk line around the area you want protected.

Ants hate salt and pepper

so sprinkle a liberal dose wherever you need to get rid of them.

Alternatively, sprinkle curry powder to get rid of ants.

If you have an infestation of ants in your wall-grown fruit,
> make a small trench under the wall
> and pour in a mixture of brine and soot.

To clear areas infested with red ants,
> try a sprinkling of whole cloves or oil
> of cloves.

To keep ants away,
> scatter spearmint leaves.

Prevent ants from coming into the house
> by planting mint by the kitchen door.

Wherever you see ants,
> sprinkle equal parts of borax and icing
> sugar.

To destroy ant eggs,
> pour boiling water on the nest.

If you want to treat mildew
　　without resorting to modern
　　fungicides, try a simple solution of
　　soapy water instead.

A sulphur spray solution will keep fungal diseases at bay.

Protect your carrots
　　by sprinkling coffee granules around
　　them.

Protect carrot plants from carrot flies
　　by surrounding them with a fence,
　　2 ft/60 cm high, made of polythene
　　or old bin liners. Carrot flies aren't
　　high flyers and so won't be able to
　　clear the fence.

Exposed colonies of mealy bugs
　　can be treated by touching them with a
　　cotton wool bud dipped in methylated
　　spirits. Repeat when necessary.

To control clubroot,
> insert a small stick of rhubarb into the
> planting hole.

To avoid Phlox eelworm,
> take root cuttings – this pest doesn't
> enter by the roots.

**Alternatively, place eggshells into the
planting hole.**

A handful of soot should also do the trick.

Leave your rose prunings on the ground;
> rabbits and cats don't like a prickly
> surface.

If rabbits are a problem,
> place worn-out footwear here and
> there in the garden. The smell of
> humans terrifies them.

Human hair deters the most determined rabbit

from nibbling garden plants. If you're a bit thin on top due to the stress of your unwelcome visitors, ask a barber or hairdresser for cuttings to sprinkle around the base of the plants.

Protect the bark of young trees

from rabbits by wrapping a 'skirt' of chicken wire round the tree. Check that it doesn't restrict the tree as it grows.

To keep rabbits out of your garden

remember:

R *Rosemary*
A *Azaleas*
B *Bluebells*
B *Box*
I *Iris*
T *Tulips*

B *Bay*
A *Asters*
N *Nasturtiums*

The red spider mite loves hot, dry conditions

so make sure you wet the floor of your greenhouse several times a day. This increases the humidity and drops the overall temperature.

Keep greenfly down

– put on some rubber gloves and go and squash them.

Keep greenfly away from your roses with this old remedy.

While it is still wet with dew, sprinkle the plant with equal quantities of sulphur and tobacco dust.

Get rid of wire worms

which can attack root vegetables by making traps. Cut potatoes into pieces and put on a wooden skewer. Bury the chunks in the ground, leaving enough of the skewer above ground to act as a marker.

To prevent aphids from attacking your apple trees,

grow nasturtiums up the trunk.

Aphids can wreck plants in hanging baskets.

Spray the baskets with soapy water to kill off the aphids.

Flea beetles can cause a lot of damage.

To get rid of them, smear a piece of bright yellow card (flea beetles *love* yellow) with grease and leave by the threatened plants.

Not all creepy crawlies are pests.

Many insects will help you wage war against pests, so encourage them. Ladybirds, spiders, lacewings, hoverflies, centipedes, ground beetles, many birds and wasps are all friends of the gardener.

Worms can spoil a beautiful lawn

– try spraying soapy water on the
turf. All the worms will come up to the
surface and you can simply remove
them to a more convenient place.

A preponderance of starlings feeding on your lawn

can indicate the presence of leather-
jackets. These are grubs that feed on
grass roots, leaving yellow patches on
the lawn. Water the grass and cover
with plastic overnight. In the morning,
the grubs will have come to the surface
and adhered to the plastic.

A 5-in/13-cm square of carpet underlay

placed round your cabbages protects
them from the root fly maggot.

Insects hate the smell of lemongrass, melissa, eucalyptus, tea tree and citronella.

Use them (in the form of essential oils)
when you're eating outside in the
summer.

Grow carnivorous plants in the greenhouse
– it's one way to keep pests at bay!

Pots of basil will keep whitefly at bay
in the greenhouse.

Keep cats off the lawn
by placing litre bottles full of water
round the area you want to protect.

Cats don't like reflections
and will steer clear of them. An old
mirror in your garden should keep
them away.

Cats behaving badly?
Have a water pistol to hand. If they
do something wrong, they get soaked
but don't associate you with the
punishment. If only men were so
easy to control!

Orange and grapefruit peel scattered round the garden
> will stop cats coming in – they hate the smell of citrus fruits.

Alternatively, cats loathe pepper
> so a judicious sprinkling will keep them away.

Don't want your garden used as a cat's loo?
> Keep the soil moist and use a moisture-retentive mulch to keep the cats away.

Burying prickly leaves just under the soil
> will deter a cat when it starts to scratch at the surface.

Prevent cats from climbing over a fence
> by spraying the wood with surgical spirit.

Angling the top of the fence inwards
> prevents cats from getting out of the garden so easily.

Keep dogs away from fence posts

by spraying the posts with unwanted perfume or aftershave.

If your dog has peed on the lawn,

pour a couple of buckets of water over the spot straight away. This will dilute the urine, making it harmless, and avoid unsightly brown patches of grass.

A prickly hedge,

like pyracanthus, will stop a neighbour's dog from digging through into your garden.

If your dog keeps digging holes in your lawn

or flowerbeds, fill a sock with pebbles. As your dog starts to dig, throw the sock out of an upstairs window so that it lands near the dog – but not on him! He won't know where it came from but will associate the unwelcome shock with digging and soon give it up.

If your dog likes rummaging around rubbish bins,
sprinkle the area with pepper to deter him.

Tree stumps can encourage fungus
if left so always try to remove them.

If your lawn is suffering from a rash of toadstools,
sweep them away with a stiff brush before the caps open and release the spores.

If your hedge is prone to silver leaf disease,
only give it its annual trim during the summer months.

Keep your garden tidy
to reduce the risk of pests and diseases. Remove any rubbish, old plants and bits and bobs – these are the natural habitats for many of your garden's enemies.

Do a regular spot check for pests and diseased leaves.

If you find any, pick them off and dispose of them carefully.

No fly spray?

Try hair spray instead. Flies hate it because it sticks their wings together – they'll soon get the message and leave you alone.

Keep flies away

– hang up bunches of elderflower.

Avoid wearing too much yellow.

Flies love the colour and can mistake you for a large flower.

Midges and flies can be a real problem when you're working outside.

Cut a sock-length off a pair of sheer tights and stretch it over a baseball cap and down over your face for a stylish protector.

If bees have taken up residence in your chimney,
> light the fire. They'll soon leave and won't risk coming back – well, would you?

Never swat a wasp.
> Many species give off a distress signal when swiped and, before you know it, you could be surrounded by its family and friends!

When a wasp lands on you,
> he's looking for something to eat. Keep very still and he'll soon realise that there is no lunch laid on, and fly off.

Attract wasps with a jar filled with jam.
> Add a splash of detergent and they'll drown more easily.

Mosquitoes hate vitamin B,
> so you could try eating copious
> amounts of vegetable extract (like
> Marmite) to stop them nibbling you
> while you're out in the garden.

For a useful mosquito deterrent,
> set out a pint of stout – it's a pleasant
> way to keep them at bay.

Drive annoying insects away from you on a summer's day
> by drinking some tonic with a slice
> of lemon. The combination of quinine
> and citrus will put off most pests.

Always clean out seedling trays and pots.
> This will cut down the risk of disease.

Use plastic pots and trays for young plants and seedlings.
> They are easier to keep clean and so
> less prone to pests and diseases.

If you live near a busy road, your plants can be affected.

A laurel hedge is more able to cope with high levels of pollution than other plants.

Marrow seeds are a most effective bait in a mousetrap.

Minimize the threat to wildlife when getting rid of rats.

Put bait down intensively for one week and then remove it.

Make sure you haven't left any little holes between or under the rocks in your rockery;

they make ideal hiding places for mice.

Put holly leaves over the trenches where you've planted sweet peas

to keep the mice away.

You think you've got mice but you're not sure?

Sprinkle flour where you believe them to be and next morning check it for footprints. If you're lucky, you will be able to track them to their hole.

Block up small holes to keep mice out.

Mice can squeeze through the tiniest hole. If you can fit a pen through a space then it's big enough for a mouse.

Deter mice from entering your home

by attaching a bristle strip to doorways.

Attract mice with their favourite titbits.

Mice prefer fruit and nut chocolate to cheese ... unless they live in Birmingham where the local rodent population have a yen for tuna (we kid you not; an earnest postgraduate student spent two years studying the phenomenon).

A humane way to catch a mouse

is to use a wide-necked jar. Fill the bottom with broken chocolate biscuits (unless you're in Birmingham) and lean a ramp against the jar. The mouse will climb in but won't be able to get out. You can then release him elsewhere.

A refreshing way to evict a mouse

is to squirt minty toothpaste around the edges of its hole. Mice don't like the smell.

One way to keep deer away

is to hang bars of soap around your garden.

Stop squirrels from digging up your newly planted bulbs

– cover the bulbs with netting.

Keep squirrels out of your bird feeder

by crushing cayenne peppers and placing them in your feeder. Squirrels hate it but the birds love it.

Squirrels loathe loud noise

so try playing heavy-metal music at full volume. The neighbours will hate it but, more importantly, so will the squirrels.

Keep squirrels and birds out of roof eaves and rafters

by screwing chicken wire into tight balls and pushing it into any awkward holes or crannies.

Keep foxes out of the garden

by spreading lion dung around the edges. You don't have to gather it yourself; just ask at the local zoo.

Don't worry if you are visited by bats

– they are friends, not enemies. They eat up to half their own weight in insects every night.

Chickens are a good way to keep down the insect population

and you get eggs as a bonus.

WATERING

....

'To a gardener there is nothing more
exasperating than a hose that just isn't
long enough.'
Cecil Roberts

Get a water butt.
Rain water is soft and much better
for your plants. It will save water
as well.

**Stop twigs, leaves and other bits and pieces
from getting into your water butt**
by securely fixing a pair of old tights
over the end of the downpipe. Clear
out regularly, especially after heavy
rainfall.

A water butt should be kept clear of algae.
Scrub it out with a stiff, long-handled
brush and soapy water.

**Make sure you can get a watering can under
the tap of a water butt.**
Raise the butt off the ground using
some old bricks if necessary.

Tap water is fine for most plants.

However, if you live in an area with a
high lime content, boil the water first,
particularly if you have a lot of lime-
hating plants (like azaleas).

**Don't use water that has been put through a
water filter**

because the chemicals in the filter can
damage your plants.

**For drainage in window-boxes use small
pine cones.**

They are great lightweight drainage
material but, even better, they can be
added to the roots without wetting the
foliage.

To water cucumber effectively,

poke four holes into the bottom of a
plastic milk bottle and bury the bottom
half in the soil. Plant your cucumber
seeds around the outside. When you
need to water or fertilize, fill up the
bottle. The moisture will go straight to
the roots without wetting the foliage.

Pink and white phlox can suffer from mildew in a dry summer
> so keep them well watered.

Watering is required every five to seven days during a period of drought
> in summer. There's no need to water every day or two just because the plants continue to droop or are not growing.

Don't waste time and energy watering lawns.
> They can be left for longer.

When you do water a dry lawn,
> spike it with a fork to ensure that the water runs down to the roots rather than evaporating on the surface.

A sign of over-watering
> is moss starting to grow on top of the potting compost.

If you have over-watered a potted plant,

take it out of its pot and repot it using
fresh potting mixture. Mix in some
sand to help with drainage.

To rescue a parched potted plant,

break up the potting mixture slightly
with a fork (being careful not to
damage the roots). Put the pot in a
bowl of water till bubbles stop rising
to the surface. Spray the leaves with
a plant spray. Drain, and leave in a
cool place.

**Be careful when watering plants in a
greenhouse or on a window-sill.**

A drop of water on a leaf can act like a
magnifying glass and cause damage to
the plant. Try to water in the early
morning or avoid getting water on the
leaves.

**Never pour water directly into the tuber
of a florist's cyclamen;**

just immerse the pot in water for
15 minutes.

Stop your wooden water butt from splitting
during a freeze; place a piece of wood in
the barrel.

**Don't blast dry compost out of hanging
baskets when you water them**
in the summer. Place half a dozen ice
cubes in a perforated food bag and place
overnight in the hanging basket. By the
morning, the plants will have been
watered.

**To make sure the soil in hanging baskets is
properly watered,**
punch holes in empty yoghurt cartons
and bury them in the middle of the
baskets. The soil then retains the
moisture and the water doesn't run
off the top.

Keep moisture in a hanging basket
by placing an old saucer in the base
of the basket when planting up.

If the compost in a hanging basket has dried out

so much that water just runs off it, add a few drops of washing-up liquid to the water. The water will then be able to penetrate the surface.

Alternatively, take the hanging basket down and put it in a bowl of water

until the compost becomes moist.

To avoid lifting heavy watering cans up to hanging baskets,

use a one-litre plastic bottle which contains just about the right amount of water for the task.

Save water.

Put pots under hanging baskets to catch any overspill of water.

To check if you've had the sprinkler on long enough,
> put an empty jam jar by the sprinkler. When there's 1 in/2.5 cm of water in the bottom, it's time to move the sprinkler.

Old bin bags surrounding a plant will help retain moisture.
> Just cover them with soil to disguise them.

Before planting a shrub,
> soak the roots in tap water. This way they get a really good drink and it's easier for you to unravel any knotted roots.

During a drought, use bath water to water the grass.
> Try not to use the water if it has bath foam or oil in it.

Water from a dishwasher or washing machine isn't suitable for the garden.

During a drought,
　leave grass clippings on the lawn to act
　as mulch.

Choose drought-tolerant plants
　such as yarrow, cotoneaster, broom,
　euonymus, lavender and lamb's ears.

Water plants in the evening
　so that the moisture has time to soak
　in overnight and not get burnt off by
　the sun.

**Prevent bacteria from building up in your
garden hose;**
　don't leave it lying around in the sun.
　The bacteria can breed really quickly in
　these conditions.

**To prevent a hose from being dragged
across flower beds,**
　drive small stakes of wood into the
　corners and edges of beds so the hose
　runs round these rather than damaging
　plants.

To ensure water gets to the roots of plants in a grow bag,

plant a plastic bottle! Cut the bottom off the bottle, make sure the cap is off and put the top end into the compost. Water through the bottle.

Hedges need to be fed and watered regularly

because they are constantly being clipped and trimmed so they tend to use up a lot of energy replacing the lost growth.

If your hedge is situated next to a road,

make sure you screen it with polythene. This will prevent the roots from taking up de-icing salt during the winter.

If you're planting a shrub in a dry spot,

make sure there's a bit of a depression in the soil round the shrub so that the water soaks down through the soil rather than running off it.

Alternatively, if your soil is wet and heavy,
don't put anything round the plant that might retain moisture. Too much water will damage the roots.

Regular watering will prevent fruit from cracking
and developing any disorders.

Water plants under a cloche with a leaky hose.
Block one end of a section of hose and make some small holes along its length. Lay the hose along a row of plants and attach the other end to a tap. Turn on the tap very gently when you need to water.

Plants that need a lot of water
are house plants that are actively growing, have budding leaves and flowers, have delicate thin leaves, are housed in fairly small pots, live in a fairly dry atmosphere (like a centrally heated house) or come from marshy areas.

To water house plants,
> use tepid water. Fill your watering can
> the night before so you don't give your
> plants a nasty cold shock.

If you are going away for a short time and are worried about your house plants,
> water them thoroughly, leave them to
> drain and then seal them in large
> plastic bags. Put some small canes or
> twigs in the compost to stop the plastic
> from touching the leaves if necessary.

To make a self-watering plant pot,
> cut a plastic bottle in half and put
> a piece of material in the spout end,
> followed by the plant. Fill the bottom
> half of the bottle with water and place
> the spout end, complete with 'wick'
> and plant on top. The material will
> soak up the water from below.

Alternatively, fill old jam jars or containers with water,

cut a hole in the lid and thread through one end of a long strip from an old pair of tights so that it reaches the bottom of the jar. Put the other end of the strip through the hole in the bottom of the plant pot. Stand the pot on top of the container.

To water plants while you are away,

stick one end of a pipe cleaner into a bowl of water and place the other end into the plant pot. The plant will then suck up the water when required.

Alternatively, fill your bath with about 1 in/2.5 cm of water

and place a thick bath towel on top. Stand your plants on the towel so they can take up water when they require it.

To give plants a really good watering,
take them into the shower with you.
A verse of 'Everything's coming up
roses' goes down well too.

To revive a bone-dry plant,
plunge it in a bucket of water and then
drain. Don't pour water over it; this
will just wash out the soil.

FLOWERS AND HOUSE PLANTS

. . . .

'It is not enough for a gardener to love flowers; he must also hate weeds.'
American proverb

Cut hollow-stemmed flowers last longer

if you turn them upside down and fill the stem with water. Place your finger over the end to keep the water in while you place them in a vase.

Cut poppies will loose sap quickly

and therefore won't last long unless you carefully singe the ends in a candle flame to create a seal.

Rubber plants leak sap when cut

so use cigarette ash to stem the sap.

House plants are used to being warm

so when you take them home, keep them in their plastic sleeves from the shop. If it's really quite cold, add an extra layer of insulation by putting the plants in a cardboard box.

Remove the stamens from lilies

to prevent the pollen from staining
clothes and furnishing fabrics. Wipe up
any pollen that falls onto polished
wood surfaces because, if left, it will
eat into the wood.

If the pollen from flowers has fallen onto your carpet or any fabric,

lift it off gently with sticky tape so that
you don't rub it in and leave an
indelible stain.

If the stem of a lily splits,

wrap it in sticky tape.

Cut flowers in the late evening

and they'll last longer.

Lily bulbs can rot in damp weather

so put a layer of gravel in the planting
hole to encourage the water to drain
away.

Alternatively, plant lily bulbs on their sides
so that water doesn't gather round
the crown of the bulb and cause it
to rot.

Repot a plant without making a mess.
Simply place the old pot inside the new
larger pot and fill the gap with soil.
Then remove the smaller pot, take the
plant out of the old pot and place it
into the hole in the new pot.

**Alternatively, use a layer or two of used
tea-bags.**

**Always keep one set of tools for house
plants and another for the garden**
so you don't run the risk of introducing
damaging diseases or pests.

**House plants grow towards the source of
light**
so turn them regularly to encourage
even growth.

Bring the shine back to dusty house plants
by wiping the leaves with a mixture of
milk and water.

**Many house plants benefit from a humid
atmosphere.**
Grouping them together is one way to
increase humidity.

**Prickly plants and cacti make a great
deterrent for would-be burglars.**
Line your window-ledges with them.

To clean a large plant with small leaves,
put it in the bath and spray it with
tepid water using the shower
attachment.

Keep plants with hairy leaves clean
by brushing away dust using a small,
soft paintbrush.

To keep cacti dust-free,
brush gently every week with a pastry
brush.

Golden barrel cactus likes a dry atmosphere.
Don't water it during its rest period in
the winter.

To repot cacti,
use old carpet scraps to hold the plant
so you don't damage your hands.

**Alternatively, fold a length of brown paper
into a wide band,**
wrap it round the cactus and hold both
ends in one hand. Pull the pot away
with the other hand.

Spotted dumb crane likes shady conditions
but keep it away from children because
its sap is poisonous.

**Herringbone plant is another one that likes
shady conditions.**
Don't leave it in too bright a light
because the bright colours of its leaves
will fade.

May-flowering peonies make beautiful cut flowers.

Don't mix daffodils with other blooms;
they release a poison which kills off other flowers.

You can use a variety of containers for cut flowers:
egg cups for pansies, a tea-cup, a copper jug, etc.

Clean vases regularly with bleach
– not washing-up liquid – to kill the bacteria residue. Flowers are dirty things!

To clean a narrow-necked vase,
fill with water and pop in a couple of denture-cleaning tablets.

To clean a smelly vase,
fill it half full of water and add a tablespoon of mustard. Shake the mixture and then leave for an hour.

Store oasis in a bucket of water
> – it should never be allowed to dry out.

Oasis should stand higher than the edge of the vase
> so you can have flowers and foliage hanging down rather than all standing to attention.

Stop oasis from floating around in a vase or a bowl
> – secure it to the bottom with double-sided tape or Blu tack.

To reuse oasis,
> turn it over and start again.

If you don't have any oasis
> put sticky tape across the top of the vase in a criss-cross pattern to form a grid to hold the flowers upright.

Use pebbles from the garden
> (make sure they are clean first) instead of oasis in the bottom of a vase.

Marbles hold flowers in place.
>If used in a glass vase, they look
>attractive too.

To make flower arranging easy
>put a wire scouring pad in the bottom
>of the vase and push the flower stems
>into the wire. The pad will last longer
>than oasis and, unlike oasis, can be
>used again even after it dries out.

**If you've bought decorative plant pots with
no drainage holes**
>and you can't put any in, make sure
>you line the base with a lot of gravel to
>help the drainage.

Alternatively, use polystyrene for drainage
>instead of gravel or stones.

If your vase has a small crack in it,
>seal the leak with a piece of soft candle
>wax.

If your vase is too big for the number of flowers you have,
> put a smaller tumbler inside the vase, fill it with water and put the flowers in that. The flowers will stand upright in the vase and won't look overwhelmed and droopy.

Never use roses or spray carnations that are in tight bud
> but make sure the petals are unfurling. Very tight buds may never open.

Use lukewarm water when arranging flowers;
> it has less oxygen in it and so you don't get many air bubbles up the stems of flowers.

To stop soil from leaking out of pots,
> line the base with some coffee filter paper.

Create a tower of flowers.
> Stack pots one on top of the other to create a dramatic display.

Add a shot of vodka to the water in your vases

– it will keep your flowers fresh for longer.

Keep the water fresh in your flower arrangement

– drop a shiny copper penny in the bottom.

A pinch of salt or sugar in a flower arrangement

slows down bacterial growth.

Prune climbing roses in September;

they bend more easily then.

Protect roses from frost by piling the soil up into a mound round the stems.

Remove once the weather improves.

To bring out really deep colours in your roses,

scatter crushed eggshells round their roots.

To get a strong blue colour in your hydrangeas,
plant something made from iron underneath.

When dead-heading long-stemmed plants,
cut back to the next growth point or set of leaves.

As rhododendron flowers fade,
remove them but be careful not to damage the plant as you do so.

Dead-head soft-stemmed plants by hand.
You get better access to the flower heads and it's easier than using secateurs.

Dahlias like a sunny open site.
After the first frost, lift the tubers, trim them and store in a frost-free dry place.

The more sweet pea flowers you pick,
the more the plants will produce.

To get the tallest sunflowers possible,
pinch out their sideshoots.

When arranging flowers,
strip off all the leaves below the water
line to prevent them rotting.

Don't put flowers next to fruit
because the fruit produces ethylene gas
which increases the maturity of the
flowers so they die more quickly.
Equally, remove dying flowers from a
bunch or arrangement because they
produce the same gas.

Smash hard woody stems
but cut soft stems before placing them
in your arrangement.

Scented flowers don't last as long as non-scented varieties
because they use up extra energy
creating the smell.

Don't place flowers in direct sunlight,
near central heating or on top of the
television. Make sure they are in a
well-ventilated part of the room.

**If your flower arrangement is going to be in
a warm room,**
keep the blooms looking lovely by
popping some ice cubes into the water
each morning.

To keep fresh tulips closed,
paint them with unbeaten egg white.

**Preserve dried flowers by spraying with hair
spray.**
It acts like an adhesive and prevents
them from falling apart.

Revitalize dried roses
by holding them over a kettle of boiling
water.

Make your own dried flowers

– use the microwave. A rose, for
example, will take three minutes on
medium power.

If you don't have a microwave,

hang the flowers upside down in the
airing cupboard for a couple of days.

To crystallize flowers,

mix one part sugar to one part water,
simmer until the sugar has dissolved.
Then put the flowers in the syrup and
simmer gently for a short while.
Remove and leave to dry.

Put a single leaf from a lemon-scented geranium

under the greaseproof paper lining
before baking a cake; it will perfume
the whole sponge.

Boiling the flowers of hollyhocks with honey, wine and water

to make a gargle was a popular remedy for sore throats in the seventeenth century.

Put marigold flowers into your bath water

to soften the water.

Love-in-a-mist (*Nigella damascena*) produces spice-scented seeds

which can be used in cooking.

Heartsease can be added to salads, sundaes and drinks.

Use rose petals in cream, ice cream, cordials and salads.

Try adding the flowers of pinks to salads or vinegar

or even using them to decorate cakes.

Nasturtiums have a strong peppery flavour
which works well in salads and
sandwiches.

Pot marigolds are so called
because they were used to flavour
soups and stews.

Crushing the petals of pot marigolds
makes a poor man's saffron; ideal for
colouring rice dishes.

When cutting flowers in the garden,
have a bucket of water with you to put
the flowers in straight away.

**Cut the stems of flowers underwater and at
an angle;**
this prevents water being blocked by an
air bubble and ensures the maximum
take-up of water.

Use a spray of foxgloves
to prolong the life of cut flower
arrangements.

Alternatively, you can make an infusion of foxglove leaves and flowers

by pouring boiling water on them and leaving overnight. Add this water to your vase of flowers the next day.

Revive droopy tulips and roses

– wrap them tightly in wet newspaper and put them in a deep bucket of water overnight.

Alternatively, revive droopy flowers with soluble aspirin in their vase

– it's a great pick-me-up.

Keep flowers fresh for longer

– add a splash of lemonade to their water.

Perk up woody-stemmed flowers

(such as roses) by putting the stems in boiling water for ten seconds, and then immediately plunging them into deep, cold water. This will move the air lock that has formed after cutting the stem.

To keep your posy of roses fresh,
> punch holes in a raw potato and insert
> each stem into a hole separately. Your
> flowers will stay fresh and pretty for a
> considerable time.

**Devon violets drink water through their
leaves**
> so always dunk them right under
> water.

**If you have a piece of lawn that isn't doing
too well,**
> why not turn it into a wild-flower area?
> Wild flowers love poor soils.

If you do plant a wild-flower area,
> don't fertilize the ground. Always wait
> until the flowers have set seed before
> cutting.

FRUIT, VEGETABLES AND HERBS

Fruit

....

'The tree is known by his fruit.'
The Bible

To remove stones from cherries,
use a hair grip stuck into a cork.

A good choice for fan-training a fruit tree
against a shady wall is a Morello cherry
tree.

Cherry trees come in two sorts
– the acid and the sweet. Plant both
kinds that flower at the same time so
that the acid one will pollinate the
sweet one (acid cherries self-fertilize).

Fruit can be grown in containers;
try strawberries, apples, pears, plums,
nectarines and any tree fruit on
developing rootstock.

Make sure your strawberries get enough water.

Put some holes in a length of hose and place this in your strawberry pot before planting up. Then just water through the hose.

Putting your strawberries under cloches

will bring the crop on earlier.

Edging a bed with neat plants

like alpine strawberries gives a sense of unity.

Once you've picked your strawberries,

don't get them near water – they'll turn soggy and tasteless.

Strawberries are a good way to clean your teeth

– they remove plaque and leave your mouth feeling fresh.

For a reviving face mask,
mash some strawberries and spread
them over your face.

Grow raspberries in a circle
to stop them casting too much shade
on other plants.

Blackberries should be grown on a wire and post system.
Train them as they grow.

Don't plant potatoes too near your apple trees
– they just don't get on together.

However, peeing on your apple trees
(especially if old men are doing the
watering) is said to encourage fruiting.

Plum trees thrive on a mixture of urine, left-over wine and some water.

Plum trees can be heavy croppers
> so prop up branches with strong sticks
> to prevent snapping.

Beating a tree
> is a sure-fire way to encourage fruit
> growth.

**Apple and pear trees need to be pollinated
by a different variety;**
> plant at least two sorts of tree that will
> flower at the same time.

If you want large apples and pears,
> thin out clusters of fruit in
> midsummer.

To grow an apple tree from a pip,
> half fill a plastic food container with
> damp compost and put several pips in
> it. Put the lid on and place somewhere
> warm (like an airing cupboard) and
> leave for several weeks.

Alternatively, drop all your apple cores in a chosen spot in the garden.
Cover them with compost occasionally and eventually one will start to grow.

To find out if a Cox's apple is ready to eat,
shake it. If the pips rattle, it's perfect.

With Golden Delicious apples,
choose the ones with more brown spots on the skin. The more spots, the more flavour.

To peel apples in half the time,
blanch them first in boiling water.

Make great teethers for babies
using dried apple rings.

Stop cut apples from going brown
– sprinkle with lemon juice.

To protect peach trees from leaf curl,
grow garlic at the base of the trunk.

Never pull stalks out of fruit;
infection may spread in the resulting
wound.

Store fruit
so that each fruit does not touch
another, and do not store different
types of fruit together.

Store apples in old shopping bags.
Put a dozen in each bag and punch a
few holes for ventilation.

To stop fruit in a bowl going mouldy,
place a piece of kitchen roll in the
bottom. It absorbs all the moisture.

**Alternatively, use a cabbage leaf in the
bottom of the fruit bowl.**

Pears are ready to eat
when the flesh round the stem
becomes soft.

Forget ships, you can grow a pear in a bottle too!

Just slip the bottle over the young fruit immediately after the blossom has fallen and secure in place. Detach both the pear and bottle carefully when the fruit is ripe. You can then fill the bottle with some strong booze, like vodka.

Pears should be stored individually on slatted trays.

An old wooden shoe rack or plate rack is ideal as long as it's thoroughly scrubbed.

A dab of sealing wax on the end of a pear stalk

will help keep the fruit fresh while you're storing it.

Don't throw old fruit away.

Pop any fruit that's gone too soft into the blender. Use the mixture as an all-over body mask and nutrient. Once you shower it off, your skin will feel really soft and you'll smell good enough to eat.

Gooseberries are the first soft fruits of the year.
> Prune them hard in the spring.

Put saucers of water under gooseberry bushes
> to keep the atmosphere moist.

Gooseberries grow well from hardwood cuttings.

To trim gooseberries,
> use baby nail clippers.

Remove fruit or berry stains from your hands
> by rubbing them with lemon juice.

Melon seeds should be kept in a warm place
> for six to eight hours before sowing.

When you cut a melon,
put it in a bowl of water. If it floats, the seeds are useless for sowing. It it sinks, they'll be fine.

To clean an aluminium pan,
boil the peel of an apple in some water. This will make it much easier to clean the pan afterwards.

Alternatively, if you have a discoloured aluminium pan,
boil up a weak solution of rhubarb or tomatoes in it. The food acids lift the stain.

Rhubarb is a great blood purifier.

Rhubarb will get rid of iron mould stains.
Soak the stain in the juice from a stem of cooked rhubarb.

To freeze fruit
use the waxed paper from the inside of cereal packets to line the trays.

To get rid of freckles,
>   follow this old recipe. Take 1 pint/
>   600 ml of white wine vinegar and put
>   it into a glass with six oak apples and
>   a few elder leaves. Set it in the sun and
>   wash your face with the mixture.

Vegetables

. . . .

*'A cauliflower is a cabbage with a
college education.'*
Mark Twain

When sowing vegetable seeds,
>   put two seeds in each hole to allow
>   for poor germination. Thin if more
>   than one seed starts to grow.

**To kick start parsnip, early carrots, onions
and parsley,**
>   sow the seeds on damp kitchen paper.
>   Leave somewhere warm until they
>   germinate. When the roots emerge,
>   wash the seeds in a sieve and then mix

into wallpaper paste. Prepare a small trench in your vegetable plot. Fill a plastic bag with the wallpaper-paste mix and cut the corner off. Go along the trench, squeezing out the paste and seeds as if you were icing a cake.

You can save space by sowing two different crops in a single row.

Mix a slow-growing crop (like parsnips or carrots) with something faster, like lettuce and radishes.

In addition, you can save space

by growing trailing varieties of marrow and squash up an arch or pergola.

Sunflowers, with runner beans growing up their stems,

make an attractive and effective screen.

Mix runner beans with sweet peas on the same support.

Pollinating insects will be attracted to the sweet peas, which will help your runner beans.

Use newspapers to line a bean trench

before filling up with compost and soil. This helps hold moisture in, especially if there's a dry spell, while the rotting paper will feed the roots.

Asparagus needs a special bed

that has been heavily manured and dug. When planting, buy one-year-old crowns and soak before putting them in the ground. Don't expect to harvest the plants for three years.

Pigeon or poultry dung in your asparagus beds

will help the vegetables grow to a larger than average size.

Vegetables can be grown in containers;

suitable ones are French beans, beetroot, radishes, tomatoes, aubergines, peppers, spring onions, lettuce and carrots.

If growing veg in containers,
make sure you choose large pots.
They're easier to look after and water
than small ones.

Keep onions away from runner beans.

Tomatoes will grow well in a window-box.

To enhance the flavour of home-grown tomatoes,
pick them just before they reach a deep
red. Put them in a drawer covered with
a cloth or paper for a few days.

To ripen tomatoes quickly,
place them in a brown paper bag along
with one ripe tomato.

Don't store tomatoes in a fridge
because they will blister.

Plant African marigolds alongside your tomatoes

to keep greenfly away.

Try planting vegetables for effect as well as food!

Oak-leafed lettuce next to purple basil or spring onions between curly, red-leafed lettuce looks stunning.

Plant flowers like poppies and love-in-a-mist in between vegetable beds.

They can survive in fairly poor soil so won't mind if the vegetables get most of the nutrients and the flowers will look pretty in between the foliage.

If you are bothered by slugs

but don't want to use slug pellets, plant a ring of cheap lettuce around your more prized varieties. Once the slugs have found some food, they won't bother looking elsewhere.

If you want easy-care vegetables,
 stick to dwarf varieties.

Peas and beans will increase the nitrogen levels in the soil
 so include them in your planting scheme.

Remember to cut peas and beans down to ground level
 once they have finished cropping. Leave the roots to add nourishment to the soil.

Peas and beans don't like garlic
 (maybe they're closet vampires) so never plant them next to each other.

New Year's Day is the time to plant broad beans
 in the South and the Midlands.

If you leave French beans on the plant until the beans develop in the pod,
> you'll have flageolet beans. Leave them even longer until they dry on the plant and you've got haricot beans which you can dry and store.

A pair of old tights slipped over a marrow
> will protect it from the birds.

Make a trench alongside your rows of vegetables.
> Water into the trench so that the moisture gets down to the roots.

To water long rows of vegetables,
> lay plastic guttering between the rows. Put small holes along its length. Pour water into the guttering.

Always water vegetables in the evening.

Don't grow large areas of one type of vegetable.

It's like hanging up a neon sign to pests saying 'Come and eat me'. Grow small areas, interspersed with other plants and vegetables.

Corn cobs are ready to pick

when the tassel at the top of the cob turns black.

Potatoes are ready to be lifted

when they flower.

Onions can be lifted with a fork

and left to dry on the ground if the weather permits.

The simplest way of storing carrots, beetroot and swedes

is to leave them in the ground. Lay some straw down for frost protection in the colder months.

If your hands are stained from beetroot or red cabbage,

rub them with a raw potato.

Drop some pieces of raw potato inside a glass vase or decanter

and swirl them around in some water until the glass becomes clean.

Look out for really purple turnips

– the more purple the turnip, the better it will taste.

If you want whiter than white cauliflower,

add some milk to the water when cooking it.

When you've harvested your cabbages,

leave the stumps to grow again. Cut them at an angle so that the rain and snow won't settle and start to rot what's left.

Cabbage can stink when it's being cooked.
A bay leaf added to the boiling water
will stop the smell without affecting
the taste of the vegetables.

Carrots are easier to scrape
if dunked in boiling water first.

Store mushrooms in a paper bag
to stop them sweating.

Mushrooms won't shrink when cooked
if you soak them in a little boiling
water first.

To cook delicious broad beans
add some chopped parsley to the water.

If you want raw onions in your salad
but are worried that they will taste too
strong, soak them in some tepid water
first.

It doesn't have to end in tears.

Store an onion in the fridge for several
hours before using and you won't cry
when you peel it.

**Alternatively, put a piece of bread in your
mouth while you chop an onion.**

If your hands smell of onions,

soak them in some milk.

**There's no need to use a sticky plaster when
you cut yourself.**

Press the inside of a clear onion skin
onto the cut. Leave it there for as long
as you can. Onion is a natural
antiseptic.

**Cucumber can be used to soothe sunburnt
skin.**

It also has a softening effect on skin.

If your lettuce has gone limp,

put it in a bowl with a piece of rinsed
coal and leave for several minutes.

Make your lettuce last longer
by cutting out the core and sprinkling
sugar into the cavity.

Tear lettuce instead of cutting it
to avoid the leaves turning brown.

Soggy tomatoes will firm up
if soaked in salty water for ten
minutes.

If you've over-cooked your vegetables,
put them in icy cold water for a few
minutes then microwave them very
briefly before serving.

**If you prepare your potatoes the night
before you need them,**
stop them becoming discoloured, by
leaving them in a pan of water along
with a small lump of coal. They will
stay looking fresh until the next day.

Store onions and garlic in the foot of some sheer tights

to keep them dry and fresh.

Herbs

'Here's flowers for you;
Hot lavender, mints, savory, marjoram;
The marigold, that goes to bed
  wi' the sun,
And with him rises weeping.'
Shakespeare

Create a herb garden

using old bricks positioned like the spokes of a wheel.

When planting herbs in a container,

plant frost-tender herbs in their own pot so you can easily replace them if they succumb to the bad weather.

Before planting parsley seeds,
pour boiling water into the trench.
This speeds up germination.

Parsley is difficult to germinate.
There's an old saying that if the
woman of a household can get the
seed to grow, then she is the true head
of the house!

**Parsley was traditionally sown on Good
Friday**
when the devil was unable to affect it.

To cut lavender for drying,
trim the stalks as the buds open
or cut back after flowers have faded.
Lightly prune the whole bush at
the same time.

Rosemary needs regular trimming.

Rosemary goes well with tripe
and steak-and-kidney pudding.

For a refreshing hair tonic,
> take a few sprigs of rosemary and cut
> up finely. Put into ½ pint/300 ml water
> and bring to the boil. Simmer for ten
> minutes and leave to get cold. To use,
> dip a piece of linen in the infusion and
> rub over your scalp.

Prune rosemary lightly;
> it will not regrow from old wood.

To keep the maximum flavour of chives,
> cut off the flower heads as soon as they
> appear.

Keep dill and fennel apart
> or they will cross-fertilize.

Mint can run amok
> if not kept under control. Plant it in its
> own container.

Camomile lawns are wonderful

and give off a fabulous smell when crushed underfoot. They need weeding by hand and like an open, sunny space.

Thyme lawns are a good idea

if you want to cover an uneven, sunny area.

Add herbs to your barbecue

for even sweeter aromas.

To stop your bins from smelling unpleasant,

throw in a few fresh herbs each time you throw something away.

Keep moths away!

Place conkers or bay leaves in your wardrobes and drawers.

Summer savory is said to improve the flavour of broad beans

and will discourage blackfly.

To dry herbs for winter,

pick just before flowering. Dry in the slow oven of an Aga or in the airing cupboard. Strip the leaves from the stems and store in airtight jars.

To dry herbs instantly,

place them in the microwave for a few seconds. This works especially well with parsley.

Use the flowers of chives

(and pansies) in salads to give colour.

Presentation is everything.

Some fresh herbs sprinkled on top of the most ordinary-looking dish will turn it into something special.

Make sure your parsley stays green

– only add it to a sauce once the liquid has boiled.

Freeze parsley on its stem in a clear plastic bag.
> When you need it, remove it from the freezer and rub it between your fingers. Your parsley is automatically chopped.

To get rid of garlic breath,
> chew some parsley.

Keep flies away
> – place fresh mint on the kitchen window-sill.

To keep watercress fresher for longer,
> immerse the leaves – but not the roots – in a jug of water.

Freshen up bad breath instantly
> by chewing two or three sprigs of watercress and a couple of grapes.

To keep water fresh,
> put a watercress leaf into a jug before filling with water.

Dill seeds make an alternative flavouring
for pickling vinegars, bread and cakes.

To clean up any spills in the oven,
sprinkle some salt and cinnamon over the spill. This stops the house from filling with that acrid smoky smell and the spill will be easy to lift off with a spatula.

To make lavender water,
simmer a handful of lavender flowers and leaves in some water for 15 minutes.

For a bath-time treat,
make your own herbal infusion. Put dried herbs in a muslin bag (you can use fresh herbs but they're not as concentrated as dried ones), tie it to the hot water tap so that the water flows over and through the bag. When the bath is ready, put the bag in the water and leave it to float around while you bathe.

For a reviving bath,
> use herbs such as mint, nettles (to boost circulation), pine (which is refreshing) and thyme.

For a relaxing bath,
> use lavender, marjoram (a great natural tranquillizer), sage (an antidote for stress) and lemon balm to relieve tension.

The leaves of angelica can be added to fruit compotes
> and cold drinks.

Borage flowers are an important ingredient in a glass of Pimms.
> The young leaves have a slight flavour of cucumber and can be chopped up and stirred into soft cheeses or salads.

To make your own herbal tea,
put one small handful of fresh herbs or one heaped teaspoon of dried herbs in a cup of boiling water. Leave to stand for five to ten minutes. Strain, and then drink the tea while it's still hot.

Soothe a nasty sore throat
– try gargling with tea made from sage leaves.

Use the same kind of sage tea to dab on to your skin
if you get a bit too much sun.

To fight the onslaught of a cold,
use rose hip berries. Crush the berries and then pour on boiling water. It makes delicious tea.

To make your own poultice,
it's best to use powdered herbs. Mix them up into a paste with hot water. Put the mixture onto some muslin or a sterile dressing and place on the affected area.

For a soothing hand lotion,
soak marigold petals in almond oil
for a couple of weeks.

For a restful night,
drink some camomile tea before bed.
It's a good idea to make a hop pillow
too; put some dried hops into a muslin
bag.

**Camomile tea is a great way to relieve
travel sickness.**
Alternatively, use fennel or ginger tea.
All three are also helpful for reducing
morning sickness.

Plant camomile next to sickly plants
to perk them up.

**Combat acne with some comfrey or
marigold ointment.**
Dabbing on lemon juice and garlic also
helps to dry up spots.

Feeling bruised and battered?

A comfrey or arnica poultice will help keep bruises down (but never apply arnica to broken skin).

For indigestion, make up some camomile or marigold tea.

If your indigestion is of a 'windy' nature, try fennel or peppermint tea. Meadowsweet tea will also bring quick relief.

If you are suffering from toothache,

try sucking on a clove next to the bad tooth (or put a drop of clove oil onto the tooth). Take sage tea as a mouthwash if your gums are bleeding. If the gums become infected, suck a clove of garlic. Sage tea is also good dabbed onto mouth ulcers.

Colds and flu don't like peppermint and elderflower tea.

If you have a headache as well, add some limeflowers.

Sage helps to relieve sore throats.

When you have got a really bad cough,
eat loads of garlic. Elderflower and
thyme tea will help ease the cough
and make your breathing easier.

If you're bunged up with a bad cold,
try inhaling the steam from thyme and
peppermint tea. Put your head over a
bowl of the tea, cover your head with a
towel and breathe deeply.

If you're really blocked solid,
try sniffing some salt water or beetroot
juice up your nose through a straw.
Sounds disgusting, doesn't it, but it
can move the blockage and bring relief.

Bunged up the other end?
Try dandelion tea to get things
moving again. Increase your intake
of fibre as well.

An alternative antiseptic cream

can be made from thyme leaves, scraped off the stem and then crushed on a board. Apply this paste to the affected area.

For sore boobs,

make up a camomile poultice. Put two tablespoons of camomile flowers into a mug of boiling water and leave it to stand for about ten minutes. Soak a flannel in the tea and then hold it gently on the affected area. Leave until the flannel has cooled.

If your nipples are sore from breastfeeding,

you can put on some marigold ointment but you should wipe it off carefully before feeding your baby.

If you suffer from hay fever,

try drinking a mixture of equal parts of elderflower and nettle tea.

When your chilblains get really bad,
squeeze fresh root ginger or lemon
juice over the unbroken skin. Eating a
lot of garlic will help to improve your
circulation as well.

After a bee sting,
brush some marigold petals onto the
affected area.

**Alternatively, rub some fresh sage leaves on
the bite or sting.**

To speed up the repair of broken bones,
take comfrey.

**Fennel seeds are good at combating
excessive flatulence.**

**Feverfew can help to reduce migraine
attacks.**
Pop a few young leaves into a sandwich
on a regular basis. Feverfew should not
be taken by pregnant women.

A natural way of darkening one's hair

is to get a handful of sage leaves, cover with a teaspoon of borax and ½ pint/300 ml of boiling water. Let this mixture grow cold and then apply it carefully to your hair with a brush. Leave for twenty minutes and wash out.

TOOLS OF THE TRADE

*'What a man needs in gardening is
a cast-iron back with a hinge on it.'*
Charles Dudley Warner

Pick fruit using an old sieve
attached to a broom handle.

Make a kneeling mat out of an old hot water bottle
stuffed with bits of material.

Alternatively, use your child's plastic sledge as a kneeling mat.

Put a couple of drops of food colouring into your rain gauge
to make it easier to read.

Sewing old shoulder pads inside your gardening trousers
will help your knees too.

Turn your electric drill into a bulb planter
with extra large drill bits. Use a 2¼-in/ 5.5-cm wide bit for small bulbs, try a 2½ in/6 cm for medium bulbs, and a 3-in/7.5-cm wide bit for larger bulbs.

Put your tools in a bucket
> and carry it round the garden with you.

Shift stains from plastic garden furniture
> with a paste made of bicarbonate of
> soda and water. Leave the paste on the
> stain for about two minutes and then
> wipe off.

**Alternatively, use lemon juice to remove
rust and stains**
> from plastic furniture.

**To preserve aluminium garden furniture
over winter,**
> lightly wipe down with cooking oil.
> Remember to wipe it off again when
> you want to use the furniture.

Stop cast iron furniture from rusting
> by wiping with olive oil or sunflower
> oil.

To restore a saggy cane or wicker chair seat,
scrub with soapy water and then rinse.
Leave the chair outside in the sun to
dry.

Put each leg of wooden furniture on a brick
to stop any rot setting in over winter.

**If you are worried about staining your
wooden table,**
put some clingfilm over the wood
before placing a cloth over it. If you are
concerned about hot dishes burning the
wood, put a blanket underneath the
tablecloth.

Save the rainforest!
Avoid buying hardwoods like
mahogany.

To remove rust from garden tools,
mix two tablespoonfuls of salt with
one tablespoonful of lemon juice.
Apply this mixture to the rust and
rub hard.

To store garden tools over winter,
grease lightly with cooking oil.

To prevent your tools from rusting,
store them in buckets of sand and oil.

Never leave tools standing on soil.
If you can't hang them up, rest them on
a wooden board wrapped in a bin bag.

Always keep your tools clean;
use an old kitchen knife to scrape
lumps of soil away.

Alternatively, use any left-over engine oil.
Leave the bottle to drain into a jar, then
brush the oil onto your garden tools or
furniture to keep them in good
condition. Wipe off before using.

**To make the handle of your spade or fork
more comfortable to hold,**
put a small section of pipe-insulating
foam over the handle. Hold it in place
with some insulating tape.

Make your own dibber.

Use a broken fork handle or a couple of bits of wood screwed together in the shape of a T.

Protect your arms when pruning old brambles or holly bushes.

Cut the tops and bottoms off old plastic sweet jars and use as arm protectors.

To make a cheap cold frame,

get a wooden apple box and cover it with a rigid piece of plastic held with twine or a strong elastic band. To shade the contents, use a piece of greenhouse shade netting or an old onion bag.

Don't throw away your old tights;

use them as hanging baskets!

Put plastic pots in the legs of old tights,

hang them in the shed and cut off the toes. The pots are then easily accessible and can be taken out (rather like the cups from a vending machine).

If you have an external tap,
make sure it doesn't drip. The water
can encourage algae growth which can
cause unattractive green marks and
dangerous slippery patches.

**Keep the tyres of your wheelbarrow free of
mud.**
If you allow mud to build up, it could
conceal sharp stones that may cause a
puncture.

Don't throw away cracked terracotta pots;
they can still be planted up. Plants
such as *Sempervivum* grow well in dry
conditions.

**Conceal broken or chipped edges on
containers**
by growing trailing plants such as
Lobelia or *Aubrietia*.

Keep drainpipes clear;
> stick a ball of galvanized wire wool
> into the opening of the drainpipe.
> This acts as a filter and stops debris
> from bunging up the pipe.

Car tyres make good plant containers.
> Stack them as high as you like for a
> really deep container.

Don't have the blades of your mower set too low.
> If you do, you could weaken the grass
> and make it more vulnerable to weeds
> and moss.

If you've just had a new bathroom put in and find yourself with an old bath
> you don't need, put it in the garden. It's
> ideal for large plants that need a big
> growing space.

If you're planting up a bottomless container
> (like an old chimney pot), put a piece of
> old net curtain across the bottom to
> keep pests out.

Little plastic crates,
>   available from supermarkets and DIY
>   stores make an ideal alternative to
>   special pond baskets.

Old watering cans, chamber pots, vegetable crates, metal drums and so on make ideal plant containers.
>   Always make sure there are enough
>   drainage holes in the bottom.

To ensure that you get an level edge when trimming a hedge,
>   tie a piece of string to two points along
>   the top.

When pruning a hedge for the first time,
>   only cut one side right back to
>   encourage new growth. In the second
>   year, trim the new growth lightly and
>   cut back the other side hard.

Protect plants from overnight frost
>   by covering with old net curtains.

Alternatively, cover plants with a couple of sheets of newspaper
   held in place by some stones.

Make your own paving slabs from concrete.
   Create the shape you want using
   two semi-rigid pieces of metal or
   plastic held together by string. Put
   this on a wooden base and pour your
   concrete mix in, making sure there
   are no gaps for it to seep out. Leave
   it for 48 hours and then untie the
   mould. Protect from frost until
   completely dry.

When making your own paving slabs,
   add concrete dye to make different
   colours.

When laying out slabs for a patio,
   dab the cement out in the shape of
   a number five on a dice. It's more
   economical and a lot easier to handle
   because there's less of it.

If you can't find a replacement for a cracked slab,

move the offending piece to a less noticeable area and swop it with a better one.

Concrete is easier to work with

if you put some washing-up liquid into the mixture.

Make sure your wheelbarrow is facing the direction you want to go before you fill it up.

It will be a lot easier to manoeuvre!

When painting wood,

make sure you get rid of any algae and other growth. Scrub it down, allow it to dry and then paint it with preservative.

Paint bamboo canes green

so that they become invisible when staked to tall plants like hollyhocks or delphiniums.

If you are putting up a wooden trellis,
>   make sure the base is at last 2–3 in/
>   5–7.5 cm above the soil to avoid damp
>   and wood rot.

**You can make a cheap fence from old
floorboards.**

**Always put a start hole in the wood before
you drill.**
>   This will stop the wood from splitting.
>   Use a bradawl to make the hole.

**Don't put screws in a row along the wood
grain**
>   because this can split the wood.

**When hammering hold the hammer near
the head,**
>   not at the other end. Make sure that
>   you use several short sharp knocks
>   rather than one almighty blow – this
>   will prevent the nail from bending.

To make a nail go into hard wood more easily,

> run it through your hair before you hammer it in. The natural grease coats the nail, allowing it to slip into the wood easily.

To stop your hammer slipping off the head of a nail,

> rub some emery paper over the hammer head.

It's quite hard to drill into thin wood

> because the wood often splits. Put a thicker piece of wood behind the thin piece and let the drill go into this thicker piece as well.

If the head of a round-headed screw has become damaged,

> use a file to make a new slot for your screwdriver.

Don't be too forceful
– if you use too much strength when driving a screw home you could end up splitting the wood.

If you want to remove a stubborn screw,
try putting a little oil on the screw head and leaving it for a while before trying to release it.

For a smoother sawing action,
rub the teeth of the saw with some candle wax.

Before you start to saw,
make a small V-shaped cut with a knife and insert the saw. Start with a backward motion before pushing the saw forward.

No plumb line?
Just hang a bunch of keys from some string instead.

Make your own screen using chicken wire.
　　You can shape it into columns or
　　stretch it across a space.

Alternatively, use willow or hazel as a screen.

Clean the upper and roof sections of your greenhouse
　　using a long-handled floor mop.

To remove stubborn marks from greenhouse glass,
　　put some methylated spirits on a cloth
　　and rub hard.

Buff up the windows of a greenhouse
　　with newspaper and a mixture
　　of water and vinegar.

To prevent birds from eating window putty in your greenhouse
　　(they're after the linseed oil), mix some
　　black pepper into the putty.

Store unused putty by rolling it tightly into a ball

> and wrapping it carefully in aluminium foil before replacing it in a tub. The putty should keep for several months like this.

Alternatively, roll it into balls and keep in jars of water.

To cut wood in a straight line,

> always use another piece of wood to guide you.

Fill old pairs of tights with compost

> to make bricks that can be used to build a retaining wall.

When building a wall,

> always spray the bricks with a hosepipe to keep the mortar wet.

To keep bricks level,

place two bricks at each end of the wall
you are building. Stretch a piece of
string between them and anchor it
with more bricks. Use the string as a
guide while you put down the next
layer of bricks.

Make your own spirit level

– use a milk bottle with a little bit of
water in it.

An old American recipe for waterproofing gardener's boots:

1 pint/600 ml boiled linseed oil,
8 oz/225 g mutton suet, 6 oz/175 g
clean beeswax, 4 oz/100 g resin. Melt
them down and mix together. While
the mixture is still warm, brush onto
new boots or shoes that are dry and
clean.

GARDEN DESIGN

....

'All gardening is landscape painting.'
Alexander Pope

Moved into a new house and don't know what to put in the garden?

Have a peek over the fence and see what's thriving next door.

Feeling generous?

Donate a plant to the neighbours to create a visual link between small gardens.

If you've inherited an overgrown, neglected garden

and don't know where to start, begin by clearing away the rubbish and cutting the lawn. Things will start to look better immediately.

Digging a new bed?

Use your hosepipe as a guide to get a great curve.

If you're taking over an established garden,

leave things for at least a year to see what the garden looks like at different times.

Draw a plan on paper first.
Take photographs of your garden
from lots of different aspects (winter
is usually a good time for this). With
a felt-tip pen, you can then sketch
in the features that you are thinking
of adding.

Never look at your garden at midday
because flowers will rarely look their
best. As the angle of light changes, the
flowers will come into their own.

Take note of where the sun reaches
and for how long.

Allow for growth.
Plants are like children ... they grow up
so make sure you've left them enough
room. Check with the nursery if you're
not sure how much space you need.

Tall plants give focus.

Plants such as cardoons, angelica or globe artichokes provide a wonderful background. Artichokes are notorious for smothering smaller neighbours so give them at least 3¼ ft/1 m² each to expand.

Not sure about a plant but can't resist it?

Pot it up in a tub if you really must have it. Don't rush to put it into the ground if you're not sure what your final plan will be.

Save money and create a stunning effect.

Buy annuals in bulk and only use two or three colours.

Don't just use herbaceous and annual plants.

Vegetables and fruit look attractive in flower beds as well. Rhubarb, runner beans, strawberries and chard, for example, all look good *and* produce fresh food for the table.

Green glass wine bottles make good edging
for your beds.

Divide a long narrow garden into a series of 'rooms'
using screens, hedges and trellis. This will make it seem wider and shorter.

In a short garden surrounded by hedge,
cut the top of the hedge slightly lower along the back of the garden to give the illusion that the end of the garden is further away than it actually is.

Alternatively, lay a path that tapers to a point away from the house.
Plant trees and shrubs along it that get gradually shorter as you move away from the house.

Planting two pots in a similar way
but one larger than the other will give the feeling of space. Put the larger one in the foreground and the smaller one to the rear.

Secret nooks and crannies
add a sense of mystery to a garden.

Plant a quick-growing climber
next to your newly erected trellis or
screen. Make sure you choose a plant
that won't outgrow the trellis.

**Clumps of bamboo make an effective
screen**
and can hide unsightly objects such
as compost heaps, dustbins and so on.

**If screening something in your garden is
difficult,**
you could make a feature of it or
highlight it in some way rather than
trying to hide it.

If you've got a post or an old tree stump
that you don't like but can't get rid of,
grow a climber up it.

Pergolas are a useful way of adding shelter
and giving an element of privacy if your
garden is overlooked.

If your garden is overlooked,
add a section of trellis to the top of
your fence and plant some evergreen
climbers.

**If you want to create a bog garden, think
big.**
A larger bog garden won't dry out as
quickly as a smaller one.

When planning a water feature,
make sure any container that you use
is frost proof.

If you're planning to build a fish pond,
don't make it too involved. Awkward
shapes can cause water to stagnate in
odd nooks and crannies.

If you are building a pond,
> make sure that animals can get in and out easily; incorporate shallow, sloping sides and rocks for them to use.

Don't situate your pond underneath trees
> because you'll have your hands full keeping the surface clear of falling leaves.

To remove blanket weed from the side of a pond,
> use a windscreen ice scraper.

During a frost, make sure you leave an air hole for your fish to breathe.
> Float a rubber ball on the surface overnight. During the day, you can take the ball away and, if possible, draw off some of the water so that oxygen can reach the surface. Never break the ice with a hammer – it's like a bomb going off at close quarters and the shock waves can kill the fish.

If you've forgotten to leave an air hole,
> heat a pan of water and hold it on top
> of the ice so it melts, leaving a perfect
> hole.

When laying paths through the garden,
> you should ensure that they are wide
> enough for one person to walk along
> with ease.

If your garden is full of curves,
> make sure your paths follow the curves
> rather than cut right through them.

A path should lead somewhere,
> even if it's just to a shed, greenhouse,
> different part of the garden, a seat or a
> statue. Paths that don't go anywhere
> look odd.

**If you have a dark path running through
your garden,**
> lighten it up by planting the borders
> with evergreens that have brightly
> variegated leaves.

To make a border look longer,
> plant brightly coloured flowers and
> plants in the foreground. Put pale
> colours at the back of the garden.

Grey plants will make a border seem longer.

**Hot, fiery-coloured flowers shorten the
distance.**

Glossy foliage perks up dull, dark corners.

**Grow copper maples, dark red roses and
pink camellias**
> in the west part of your garden to catch
> the rays of the setting sun.

If you want a patio,
> you will need a space at least 8 ft × 8 ft/
> 2.5 m × 2.5 m. This is enough space to
> accommodate a standard garden table
> and four chairs.

If your patio is too small,
你 you can extend it by simply laying
some gravel and surrounding it with
brick.

If your patio doesn't get enough sun,
consider pruning, even moving, a tree
or painting the surrounding walls
white.

Use mirrors to enlarge a small garden.

**Old bailer twine makes a bright and cheap
way to mark out your garden.**

Get rid of boring stretches of grass.
Alter the shape by adding curves or
making an island bed.

**Alternatively, create a focal point by
planting a specimen tree.**

When it comes to looking after your lawn,
save yourself a lot of extra effort when mowing – don't break the lawn up with too many flower beds.

Trimming the edge of the lawn
becomes a thing of the past if you lay a border of flat paving stones flush with the turf between the flower bed and the lawn.

To make curves in the edge of the lawn,
drive a small stake into the ground and attach some string to it. Attach a funnel filled with sand to the other end, pull the string taut and allow the sand to trickle out as you draw an even curve.

When planting a tree in a lawn,
leave a circle of earth three to four times the diameter of the rootball. You can feed a tree more easily this way and it prevents direct competition with the grass.

If you want something screening from spring to autumn,

plant a deciduous tree.

Bulbs that flower in the spring are a nice feature

to plant under a tree. They don't have to worry about not getting enough sun because the tree doesn't cast much shade at this time.

If you want to put a bench or seat round a tree,

make sure you leave enough room for the trunk to expand.

Island beds break up big expanses of grass

but make sure the proportions are in keeping with the size of the lawn.

A trellis arch can divide a garden into two.

Plant an evergreen shrub either side to mark the boundary.

A curved lawn gives the garden a more casual look

while straight edges are suitable for a formal look.

An ornamental divider breaks up a long lawn.

You may choose a statue, urn, small fence, pergola or arch.

When building an archway,

make sure it's wide enough for two people to walk through and tall enough to take into account the kind of plants you're going to grow up it.

Make a quick and easy arch for a lightweight plant.

Get a length of old hosepipe and stop up the ends. Push both ends into the ground and you have an instant arch.

Fast-growing climbers will cover an archway really quickly

– try *Ipomea*, *Eccremocarpus scaber* and *Thunbergia alta*.

Alternatively, runner beans make an attractive edible arch.

If you want to cover an archway with roses,
choose a rambler rather than a climber. Ramblers are more flexible.

When putting up a shed or greenhouse,
choose your site carefully. You don't want to create a wind tunnel and damage your plants.

Where wind is a problem,
a hedge is better than a wall. Hedges disrupt the wind, creating calm, whereas wind simply rushes over and around walls.

Noise is a nuisance in built-up areas.
A solid hedge will block out quite a lot of noise. Even a fairly big tree will reduce road noise.

Well-planted pergolas will reduce overhead aircraft noise.

Alternatively, rustling trees, water and birds
will detract from other more
unpleasant noise.

Roses can make excellent hedges;
they deter intruders with their sharp
thorns, are attractive in the autumn
and make great homes for wildlife.
Rugosa roses are the best kind for
hedging.

**Camellias are a good choice for winter
interest;**
they have dark, glossy evergreen
leaves and flower in the early
spring.

**Put herbaceous borders at right angles to
the house**
so that you get a massed effect of
flowers. It's harder to spot gaps from
this viewpoint too.

Perk up a dull brick wall by painting it,
growing fruit trees or climbers against
it, adding a mirror or being really
creative and painting a mural.

If you're starting a new lawn,
cut old tyres in half and place them
under the soil (at least 1 ft/30 cm below
the surface, and at 3 ft/90 cm intervals)
to act as reservoirs.

**Autumn and spring are the best times to lay
a new lawn**
because the grass will re-establish itself
quickly. Always water a new lawn
regularly.

For lawns that suffer from heavy use,
add finely chopped car tyres to the top
dressing.

If your lawn has too many dips and hollows,

it might be due to bad drainage (check for moss – this is a good indicator of poor drainage). Use a lot of grit in the soil that you use to fill the hollows out.

Uneven areas can also be caused by buried tree roots or lumps of debris.

Dig out whatever is causing the problem and replace it with topsoil.

When sinking slabs into the lawn,

make sure that they are deep enough so that the lawnmower runs over them easily.

Stepping stones make an ideal alternative pathway across a lawn.

To break up a long flight of steps,

place terracotta pots along the edge of the steps.

Alternatively, soften the line of steps
by growing plants along the treads.
Make sure you use plants that aren't
going to take over.

You can make a flight of steps look more formal
by placing two matching containers of
plants either side of the bottom or top
step. Plants such as rose trees, bay
trees, box plants or spiralling wire with
ivy growing up it are ideal.

If your garden slopes away from the house,
put progressively taller shrubs down
the slope – an effective way of seeing
more garden.

Direct night lights away from your garden
and towards nearby trees for a magical
green backdrop.

To absorb chemicals from the air,
>   try planting azaleas (to counteract
>   formaldehyde), English ivy (for
>   benzene) and Peace Lily (for
>   trichloroethylene). Chemicals
>   like these are found in paints
>   and varnishes.

**Age a new statue or pot by rubbing over
with natural yoghurt.**
>   Within a few weeks, algae and bacteria
>   will have begun to age it.

Alternatively, weather a new terracotta pot
>   by rubbing it with fresh parsley.

**Use yoghurt or liquid manure to age your
patio.**
>   Just paint it on and leave for a while.

**Use old car tyres to make simple, cheap
plant holders**
>   for your patio.

You don't have to put plants in containers.

If they are interesting shapes, they can be a focal point in their own right.

Group several plants together in a container,

especially ones with interesting foliage or when they're in full flower. Choose plants that need similar growing conditions.

When grouping container-grown plants together,

choose pots that are of a similar shape or size. If you don't have the same sort of containers, make sure that you put similar plants in them in order to link the group together.

Raised beds are a good way of adding interest to a patio.

If you are using bricks, make sure they are frost proof and that they blend into their surroundings.

Alternatively, use concrete blocks to make a raised bed.

If you want to grow lime-hating plants, line the sides of the bed with heavy duty polythene.

Always put drainage holes in the bottom of raised beds.

Stain your fences a variety of colours for a stunning effect.

A cheap way to preserve your fence

is to paint it with engine oil from your car.

A dense trellis is more beneficial to plants than fencing

because it creates an air flow through the garden.

When fixing trellis to the wall,

always set it slightly away from the wall so that air can circulate round the plants. Position small wooden blocks or old cotton reels between the trellis and the wall, as you nail the trellis in position.

Fences need to be checked regularly and patched up.

If a post rots at its base, sink a new one beside it and bolt the two together.

If your fence leans,

large wooden struts wedged against the posts at angles will bring it back upright. Once plants grow around the struts, they'll be hidden.

Got a garden with a slope like the side of Everest?

Cut terraces into the slope and build retaining walls to keep the soil in place.

To keep soil in place on a slope,
    use netting pegged into the ground.

Don't creosote a fence if you want to grow climbers up it
    because it takes time for the fumes to die away.

Grow a variety of climbers up a wall;
    if they have different flowering times, you will always have something attractive to look at.

Hide hanging basket chains
    by growing trailing plants up them.

If you've got a pile of unwanted rubble,
    don't bother to move it. Plant a climber next to it to disguise it, such as rose or clematis. If the rubble includes concrete, don't use lime-hating plants.

Don't put plants too near a wall
   – a climber should be about 1 ft/
   30 cm from the wall while shrubs
   can be anything up to 3 ft/90 cm away.

To renovate discoloured brickwork,
   use an old brick of the same colour.
   Soak the old brick in a bucket of water
   and then rub it over the damaged area.

**Combine different materials for a more
interesting effect:**
   slabs, bricks, paving stones, gravel and
   cobblestones can all be mixed and
   matched.

To achieve an even pointing finish,
   use a piece of old garden hose. Push it
   against the mortar to get the desired
   result.

Plant compact annuals between patio slabs
   to soften the look of your patio.

Don't use plants with a vigorous root system in a patio

– they may displace the slabs in the future.

Remove broken slabs or whole sections of your patio

and plant directly into the soil. Make sure that you prepare the soil carefully; it won't have had many nutrients and will probably be severely compacted.

To age new bricks,

brush them with milk.

When building a rock garden,

just mimic nature. Build the rockery up in layers, tilting the stones here and there.

If you want a rock garden but have heavy clay,

dig in a layer of brick rubble 16 in/ 40 cm below the soil's surface to ensure good drainage.

In winter, put an old plate on top of your hanging basket

and use it as a bird table. This is also cat proof.

A wooden frame will support a trellis

more effectively than a plastic one and it will look better and last longer. Use pressure-treated timber for your support.

Use galvanized nails and screws when fitting a trellis

to prevent rust from forming.

Drill a pilot hole into wood so that it will accept a screw.

A pilot hole is a smaller hole than the actual screw size.

Don't be a square when it comes to choosing the shape of your trellis.

They come in all sorts of shapes and sizes nowadays so you don't have to go for the more traditional look.

For a dramatic effect, paint your trellis with coloured wood preservative.

You can choose something that either complements your colour scheme or strongly contrasts with it.

Always build a barbecue a little larger than you think you'll need.

You'll be glad you did when you hold a big party.

Don't build a barbecue too near the house:

you want to cook food, not smoke out your home.

Don't put it too near your neighbour's fence either:

you want to remain on good terms with them!

When building your own barbecue,

make sure you can fit standard-sized metal grilling racks so that they can be replaced easily.

Avoid placing a barbecue under trees
which may be scorched badly by the
heat.

**Make your barbecue double up as an
incinerator in the winter.**
Just lift off the metal grilling rack and
secure it to the front of the barbecue so
that it will hold in the leaves and
rubbish that you're going to burn.

GREEN FINGERS

. . . .

'The garden that is finished is dead.'
H. E. Bates

To test if the soil was warm enough for sowing,

gardeners of old would remove their trousers and sit on it. If you don't want to bare all, test the ground with your elbow as you would a baby's bath water.

Take note of which part of the garden the sun reaches

and for how long to help your planting plan.

A climbing hydrangea is quite happy

in an exposed shady site.

Protect tender perennials from frost

by lining a hanging basket with straw and placing it over the top of the plants.

Check your insurance policy if you have window boxes or hanging baskets.

Are you covered if they fall and damage someone or something?

Always push – never pull – your wheelbarrow;
> you have more control this way.

The best time to buy plants is in the spring
> because you can get a good idea about their health by checking their foliage.

When buying plants,
> there's nothing wrong with taking the plant out of its pot and checking its root system.

Try not to buy plants that have moss, algae or weeds growing in their compost.
> This could mean that the plants have been in their pots for too long.

When buying shrubs,
> look for young, small plants. They will grow more rapidly and establish themselves more successfully than larger shrubs ... and they'll probably be cheaper too.

If you come across a shrub for sale that's been pruned in an odd fashion, don't
touch it. It probably means that the plant was damaged in some way.

Don't buy new heather plants;
just place a heap of cuttings compost in the centre of your old heather plant and moisten. New heather roots will start to form in about six months' time.

Bubble wrap is an effective way to insulate your greenhouse.
With an aluminium frame, use clips to attach the wrap and in a wooden greenhouse, pin the wrap to the frame. Cover the ventilators separately so they can still be opened.

To keep an eye on your greenhouse in winter,
place a small dish of water inside and you'll know when the temperature reaches freezing.

When sweeping up the leaves in autumn,
first check which way the wind is
blowing and then sweep with the wind.

When growing azaleas and rhododendrons,
plant some foxgloves next to them.
They help to keep the other plants
healthy.

Rock plants like to be divided
every four or five years.

Equally, day lilies like to be divided
up every four or five years.

Cover yourself before moving a plant
– take some cuttings just in case the
move doesn't work.

When taking cuttings,
put them in a plastic bag until you are
ready to plant them up.

To stimulate a cutting and encourage root formation,
> cut a sliver of bark from one side of the cutting's base.

Snow can damage trees.
> Protect conifers and similarly densely branched trees by tying the branches together with wire or rope.

Spank your trees to stimulate their growth.

Elder trees were believed to protect houses from witches;
> they are also good at seeding themselves in awkward spots.

The mulberry tree never puts out leaves until the danger of frost is past;
> that's probably why it was also known as the 'wise tree'.

If you keep birds,
> look in the garden for the perfect perch.
> Don't just stick in a bit of dowelling
> and be done with it. Birds need
> different shapes and diameters of perch
> in order to exercise their feet. Sticks
> such as bamboo or willow that have
> varying diameters are best.

Love birds adore having strips of willow bark in their nesting boxes.

Collect berries in the autumn
> and then freeze them to keep as treats
> for your birds all year round.

If you keep bees,
> make sure you've got a lot of ivy
> around. The winter flowers of ivy
> are an important source of nectar for
> late-flying insects.

If a climber has grown in too symmetrical a fashion,
> trim it back unevenly to give it a more
> informal outline.

...grown plants warm over
...rap before

To stop thieves walking off with your planters and tubs,

> put several stones in the bottom of each tub before filling and planting. They will then be too heavy to lift.

If you want to create a garden on a balcony or roof,

> always check that it can take the added weight.

Use large containers

> which can take as many plants as lots of small pots but won't dry out as quickly.

If you live in a high-rise flat,

> only plant low-growing plants in your window box. Make sure they are anchored firmly in the soil to protect them from the wind.

Don't replace a ~~~ ...ub in the same
something. y pick up the same disease.
If ~

**Use a staple gun to fix climbing plants to a
fence.**

When training young plants,
use a bit of exhaust putty or Blu tack.

The best support for clematis is nylon wire
wrapped round sheds, posts and tree
trunks.

Prune late-flowering clematis hard.
Early varieties won't need such tough
treatment.

Pinch out the tips of ivy
to encourage bushiness.

...r lawn starts to look a bit

...urn it

Gaps in the lawn?
If you can't be bothered to start all over again, simply fill in the gaps with tea-bags.

If your soil is heavy,
stand on a board when digging it to avoid compacting it further.

If you have clay soil, use a fork not a spade.
A spade can seal the edges and make it hard for water to drain through.

Box is often used to edge lawns and paths.
One problem is that after trimming, it can smell a bit 'catty'. One remedy is to leave hard limestones in some water for three to four hours and then water the box with this water.

A pansy is a ~~~~~~~ a viola.
necessari~~~

A bulb is made up of swollen leaf bases

while a corm is similar but made up of a swollen stem.

When storing bulbs, make sure that they are kept dry.

Put them on dry sand or newspaper so that they're not touching each other.

To check if a bulb is healthy, give it a squeeze.

It should be firm to the touch.

Some people are allergic to the scales on bulbs

so wear gloves when handling hyacinth, iris, narcissus, bluebell and tulip bulbs.

Recycle your guinea pig's droppings and left-over food.

Sprinkle them on the garden to grow sprouted oats which, when peeled, can be fed back to him.

If you get blood on a sheepskin coat,

just sprinkle potting compost on it. It works like blotting paper. Leave it overnight and brush it off in the morning.

To remove grass stains

place a clean cloth under the fabric and dab another cloth in methylated spirits. Clean the stain with a small circular movement, working from the centre outwards.

Don't do too much digging and moving of plants in winter;

you'll only run the risk of damaging their roots and your back. Wait until spring.

To keep warm while you're working in the garden,
> wear lots of thin layers rather than a few bulky ones. You can then take layers off as you wish.

It's more hygienic if the layer next to your skin is cotton.

If you have cold feet, wear a hat
> – you lose most of your body heat through your head.

Don't put wet boots in front of the fire
> because this makes them really stiff and they may even shrink. Stuff them with newspaper instead and leave them in a well-ventilated spot to dry out.

You can store a plant for a while before planting it.
> Evergreen shrubs and conifers can stay in a sheltered spot to protect them from extreme temperatures.

Bare root plants can be left in an unheated shed or garage

for a few days before planting. Cover the roots loosely with an old sack or polythene bag so they don't dry out.

Hang an old curtain over the shed door

to keep draughts out.

If you are planning to store a plant for a while,

don't feed it. You want it to rest not get all stimulated!

Transporting young plants can be difficult.

Try using cereal boxes. Cut the box in half lengthwise. Punch a few holes in the bottom and then slip over the top of the seedling tray.

Protect a small plant from the sun

by covering it with a large empty flowerpot before the temperature starts to rise.

Twigs make good supports for multi-stemmed plants.

Place chicken wire (formed into mounds) over plants like phlox,
> hardy geraniums and dianthus when they're dormant. They will then grow up through the wire which becomes their support system and you won't have to stake them out later on.

Avoid clipping or trimming your hedge during the nesting season.
> Wait for at least two weeks until the birds have flown the nest. The hedge can wait that little bit longer and you're doing your bit for wildlife.

Always clip hedges so that the upper surface slopes.
> This will stop snow from collecting on top and damaging the shape of the hedge.

After trimming your garden hedge,
   leave the cuttings. When you mow
   your lawn, the twigs and leaves can be
   collected with the grass cuttings.

Prune a pyracanthus in stages
   and you will have berries in the
   autumn. Cut some stems in early
   spring and others after flowering.

**Make sure you have a ready supply of
plants for next year;**
   pot cuttings from perennials in late
   summer.

Don't be too tidy;
   leave some areas for helpful garden
   animals to hide in.

Try not to walk on frost-covered grass
   because you can damage the blades,
   making it vulnerable to disease.

Add a drop of brandy to your watering can
    so that you can be sure your lawn
    comes up half cut.

Put soap under your finger nails
    before gardening. They'll be much
    easier to clean afterwards.

Clean grubby nails with minty toothpaste
    (this is especially effective for
    smokers).

Always protect your hands
    – wear gloves.

Get hands clean after a hard day's gardening
    with soap, water and sugar.

Salt baths help to heal any wounds or scratches on the skin.
    Add a cup of salt to the bath water.

Don't wash your hands in very hot water
because it strips the skin of its natural oils. Warm water and a gentle soap is just as effective. Always apply hand cream after you've got your hands wet.

If your hands become stained or discoloured,
rub the skin with half a lemon. Rinse off and dry your hands carefully, then massage in some hand cream because lemon has a drying effect on the skin.

For heavy duty hand cream,
mix virgin olive oil and petroleum jelly together. Rub the mixture into your hands and then put them in freezer bags. Sit and have a cuppa or read the paper while your hands absorb the benefits of this perfect conditioner.

If you've been on your feet all day,
give them a treat. A cup of baking soda or Epsom salts dissolved in a bowl of warm water makes a wonderful foot bath.

Try not to wear wellies for any great length of time.

Your feet won't benefit from it and they'll smell awful as well.

Sitting on the ground or stone can be wet and cold.

Make your own insulated cushion from a sheet of kitchen foil sandwiched between two pieces of foam.

A newly planted pond will invariably turn bright green with algae at first.

Be patient. Allow the natural balance to establish itself before you rush in with drastic solutions.

If you want fish in your pond,

introduce them to the idea gently. Float the plastic bag that they've been transported in on the surface of the pond water for an hour. The temperature of the water in the bag will equalize gradually; you can then release the fish into their new home.

Always handle plants by the soil or leaves,
never by the stems.

To get rid of nasty splinters,
mash up some bread and mix with
water until it's gooey. Place onto the
splinter which should then be drawn
out by the paste.

**If you run out of starch and you've got
bluebells in your garden,**
you can use the juice from the white
part of the stems as a substitute.

**Boiled and mashed ivy leaves are perfect for
cleaning black silk.**

**Potato water is better for washing pale
coloured silks.**

Create your own brown paint
by sieving soil and then cooking it in a
saucepan. Mix with acrylic paint to get
a lovely deep colour.

Cheap effective charcoal sticks
can be made by wrapping willow tree
branches in tin foil and baking them in
the oven.

When holding a garden party,
fill a child's paddling pool with ice to
keep bottles cold.

If you're holding a children's party outside,
get your children to decorate some old
bed sheets and use them to sit on and
have a picnic.

For natural dyes,
use elderberry leaves for green, the
flowers for yellow and the berries for
purple.

The old-fashioned pink, Sops in Wine,
was used to flavour mulled wine.

Make your own toothpaste.

Take some juniper twigs and leaves
when the sap is full. Dry them in the
airing cupboard. Place them on a large
metal tray and set fire to them. The
resulting ash can be used to clean your
teeth.

Remove grass stains from clothing

by hanging the washed item with the
stain directly facing the sun. The rays
will remove the chlorophyll.

A good cure for dandruff

is to put about ten or twelve stinging
nettle heads into a bowl. Pour boiling
water over them and leave to cool.
Strain so that any bits are removed.
The left-over liquid can be used as a
final rinse after shampooing.

To get rid of warts,

rub them with the milky sap from
a dandelion stalk.

To make rose water,

cover 2 lbs/1 kg of rose petals (from scented bushes – cabbage or damask are best) with cold soft water and bring slowly to the boil. Simmer for a few minutes and then strain. To intensify the scent, add a few drops of oil of geranium.

One of the best face creams is rose cream.

Melt 2lb/1 kg of fresh lard (not salted) in a large basin over a saucepan of boiling water. When it has melted, add 2 lb/1 kg of scented rose petals (red ones if possible) and mix. Keep the mixture over the pan of boiling water all day, stirring frequently. Pass through a sieve. The next day, melt the fat as before and add 1 lb/450 g of fresh rose petals. Repeat the process three or four times. After the last time, pour the fat into small pots, cover with paper and tie down. The cream will last for a year.

Quince lotion was thought to whiten the skin.

Put 7 pints/4 litres of quince blossoms in a pan, cover with cold water and simmer for an hour. Cut two cucumbers into thin slices, chop finely and add to the quince blossom mixture. Boil for five minutes. Strain through muslin and, when cold, put into bottles and tie down. To use the quince lotion, smear on face and hands and leave for 15 minutes before washing off.

If you have to replace or treat a section of fence,

do so in the autumn or winter so that you don't damage plants.

Give the birds a treat

– place small piles of wood and branches round your garden. These 'islands' will soon fill up with insects, providing a welcome source of food for the birds.

If you suffer from hay fever,

> try avoiding pollen rich flowers and go for something else – hostas are a good alternative.

Ensure that your hedges are stocked with fruits

> for birds and mammals – trim the hedges in winter.

You can be buried on your own land

> but you have to get permission from the local planning department and you must inform the environmental health officer.

INDEX